Calling Planet Earth: Close Encounters with Sun Ra

Calling Planet Earth: Close Encounters with Sun Ra

by

Bob Mielke

Golden Antelope Press
715 E. McPherson
Kirksville, Missouri 63501
2019

Copyright ©2019 by Bob Mielke. Cover design by Russell Nelson.

Cover image of Sun Ra's Discipline 27-11 album cover is used with permission of Adam Abraham. It is located in the Alton Abraham Collection at the University of Chicago Special Collections Research Center. It has been adapted for this book by Russell Nelson.

Portions of this book are reprinted from Dr. Mielke's previous book, *Adventures In Avant Pop* (Golden Antelope Press, 2013).

All rights reserved. No portion of this publication may be duplicated in any way without the expressed written consent of the publisher, except in the form of brief excerpts or quotations for review purposes.

ISBN   978-1-936135-33-2 (1-936135-33-7)

Library of Congress Control Number: 2019956431

Published by:
Golden Antelope Press
715 E. McPherson
Kirksville, Missouri 63501

Available at:
Golden Antelope Press
715 E. McPherson
Kirksville, Missouri, 63501
Phone: (660) 665-0273
http://www.goldenantelope.com
Email: ndelmoni@gmail.com

Lovingly dedicated to Grace and the memory of three teachers and friends who taught me about theater: Carolyn Asp, Dale Randall, and Arnie Preussner

Contents

I Introduction   1

We Travel Ra's Spaceways   3
    Cosmo Sun Connection to the Alter-Destiny 3
    But Is It Jazz? 9
    But Is It Avant-Pop? 12
    Where Is Sun Ra Coming From, Besides Saturn? 17
    Was Sun Ra From Saturn? 21
    Transition 31

II Discipline-27-II   33

Discipline 27-II Set-Up   35
    Dramatis Personae 36
    Scenes in the Play 37
       Prologue 37
       Act One 37
       Act Two 37
    Discipline 27-II: A Cosmo-Drama in Two Acts 37
       Induction / introduction to the play: 37
       In the lobby: 37
       On the stage: 39

Prologue   41

Act One   45
    Scene 1 45
    Scene 2 48
    Scene 3 50
    Scene 4: Peacock Club, Chicago 1947 54
    Scene 5: Sun Ra's Apartment, Chicago 1955 56

Scene 6: same, 1960 63

Act Two   **65**
Scene 6: New York, Slug's, 1969 65
Scene 2: Philadelphia, House of Ra, 1969 71
Scene 3: Orlando, 1969 75

Notes for the Play   **79**

III   Critical Remarks   83

Some Omniversal Listening Suggestions   **87**
The Chicago Years (1948 - 1960) 89
The New York Years (1961-1968) 90
The Philadelphia Years and the Arkestra on World Tour (1968-1992) 98
    Studio Work (1968-1970) 98
    First European and African Tours (1970-71) 100
    Stateside Live Appearances, Studio Work, and a Jaunt to
        Paris (1970-71) 103
    Back in Europe (1976) 109
    The Late Seventies: Outburst of Productivity 110
    The 1980s 116
    Final Recordings, or, Sun Ra Leaves Earth 121
Posthumous Discoveries and Tributes 123
    Discoveries 123
    Tributes 136

Why Sun Ra Matters   **141**

Notes and Works Cited   **149**
Works Cited 155

Appendix: Musical Highlights from The Complete Detroit Jazz Center Residency, December 26, 1980 - January 1, 1981   **157**

Afterword: What's New?   **171**

Part I

Introduction

We Travel Ra's Spaceways

Cosmo Sun Connection to the Alter-Destiny

The first and only time I ever heard Sun Ra's music on the radio (unless I played it on my own campus radio shows) was in late May or early June of 1993. The place was Washington, D. C.; the station was the then-incredibly-hip Radio Pacifica. My delight turned to sorrow when I heard a second Ra tune played in a row. "He's passed on," I immediately and correctly concluded. When I saw Sun Ra and his Arkestra a few years earlier at the Artist's Glam Slam nightclub in Minneapolis, Ra was wheelchair-bound and frail. I knew he was feeling poorly. It took his departure from Earth to get him some brief radio exposure.

Because of his sub-underground status, every Ra fan has a story about how they first came to discover his work, a veritable secret musical history of the omniverse (which is bigger than the universe, in case you're wondering). Until the end of his career, the only way his home label El Saturn got distributed was by mail order, hand delivery to specialty record stores or off the bandstand at concerts (Szwed 170). Like many midwestern Ra fans, I got my first exposure to the Man from Saturn in a cut-out record bin where I acquired *The Solar-Myth Approach, Volume 2* on the French Actuel label for a buck or two in the early seventies. What made a nice caucasoid high-schooler like me buy an album with a black guy on the cover wearing a Mexican hat and some freaky orange glasses with only tiny slits to see through? On the back he and his band were clad in capes and bizarre jerry-rigged helmets and *dashikis*; nowhere was there any listing of the musical contents of the recording. The abundance of reeds suggested that they could be playing jazz, although the record might have been in the rock bin. I didn't normally check the jazz section back then; Ra was my first jazz purchase! So how did curiosity catch this particular cat?

I grew up listening to some pretty god-awful music. My older parents were big fans of Lawrence Welk, a fourth remove from decent jazz (Ellington to Goodman to Glenn Miller to Welk's fusion of big band with mitteleuropic ethnic effects like the polka). They also liked Bob Kames's Hawaiian-inflected organ records. My brother snuck off to hear Ahmad Jamal and George Shearing in Chicago, but his record club purchases stuck to Ferrante and Teicher, Martin Denny (I unapologetically grooved and groove to *Quiet Village*), the soundtrack to *West Side Story* and an early album by Peter, Paul and Mary (admittedly big improvements on the parental selections). My sister was hippest with Elvis (on 45s only, alas—the problem with being in the Columbia record club vs. RCA). I forget which sibling had *Trini Lopez Live at the Purple Onion*, but both liked it. The only Negroes allowed in our white-bread house (ironically in an African-American ghetto in the making) were the Platters and Nat King Cole. You get the picture.

Needless to say, the British couldn't have invaded too soon. Even there I got off on the wrong foot. I was taking a bath when the Beatles first played Ed Sullivan, so I had no way of knowing my neighbor and playmate Duane Kirshner was completely full of shit when he told me that the Dave Clark Five were destined to contribute more to western civilization. The good news is that I learned after I heard my first Beatles record TO TRUST MY OWN EARS, the secret to music appreciation when all is said and done. The bad news is that Duane's love of the DC5 proved to be the harbinger of a series of existential wrong turns for him. I lost track when he dropped out of my high school.

Once I got the Beatles issue straightened out, I took the journey of many fellow boomers and watched them evolve from a rocking teen combo to avant-popists in their own right with the increasing experimentation that began with *Rubber Soul*. Soon I was also investigating the new psychedelia: the Moody Blues, King Crimson, Pink Floyd and so many others. An even more crucial development for my musical ear was my appreciation of Stanley Kubrick's 1968 movie *2001: A Space Odyssey*, which led me to purchase the soundtrack recording. Luckily, and thanks to tolerant music teachers, I had an unbiased ear. I didn't know the cardinal rule of musical socialization in western culture: that consonance sounds good and pretty and dissonance sounds evil and ugly. To me, this has always made as much logical sense as a color preference: green is beautiful and purple is ugly. Consonance and dissonance were just different musical effects, but either could be wonderful depending upon their use. So I intuitively loved the three compositions by Hungarian composer Gyorgy Ligeti on the 2001 soundtrack. This was real "space music," conveying the feel of contact with the alien. Unquestionably, it was the most adventurous record in my house—and the one that best prepared me to appreciate Sun Ra.

The final piece of the puzzle was a series of references to Sun Ra (even a cover story) in *Rolling Stone*. At the time, I was assisting a peer who was in the business of providing light shows for Milwaukee bands. I was intrigued to learn that Ra was doing light shows and space spectacles long before the acid rock bands emerged on the scene. *Rolling Stone* gave him credit for being an innovator in this regard, as well as being the earliest user of exotic electronic keyboards. In fact, Ra's earliest recording "Deep Purple" (between 1948 and 1953, depending on your sources) uses a Solovox (an odd proto-synthesizer electronic keyboard [Corbett 164, Szwed 427]). Thirdly, Ra and his band wore exotic costumes in Chicago in the 1950s, long before Arthur Brown and Doctor John kicked psychedelic fashions up a notch with their regal robes. Sun Ra, according to *Rolling Stone*, was a secret progenitor of the new counterculture. Even as Pat Boone homogenized Little Richard a decade earlier, white entrepreneurs had seen the Ra spectacle in Chicago and New York (especially at Slug's tavern every Monday night) and adapted it for new scenes like the UFO club in London.

This information led me to buy the Ra cutout album when I saw it; I needed to *hear* this guy, and buying the record seemed like the only way that could happen. But it was my fondness for Ligeti that kept my ears open when I put it on the turntable. The first track on *The Solar-Myth Approach, Volume 2* is "The Utter Nots," an uncompromising example of Ra's space music. It sounds like a round of free solos, but Ra explained that he had to compose those levels of chaos (mere improvisation couldn't guarantee results that wild!). The reed instruments are burning the zoo down, then drums and piano come in, Marshall Allen on alto saxophone with frenzied percussion backing, Ronnie Boykins on bowed bass. To bring things to a climax, Ra uses the "space key" or "space chord": "a collectively improvised tone cluster at high volume" (Szwed 214). (In concert, he could use this as an all-purpose transitional device for the program.) It sounded like nothing I had ever heard before, but I liked its fierce energy and curious mixture of freedom and control. This band knew what it was doing; there was a structure to the sonic extravagance. On first listens, I couldn't tell for sure if this was programmatic science fiction music portraying a world of chaos and negation best not spoken of ("The Utter Nots," after all, is a pun) or just some funky African-Americans baiting the bourgeoisie with signifying sounds—a logical extension of James Brown on the TAMI show. After all, I could hear even then the abundant humor in Ra's music. John Gilmore's falsetto squeaks on tenor sax and Pat Patrick's honking on the baritone create risible as well as profound effects (lessons not lost on emergent Chicago musicians like the Art Ensemble of Chicago). The Arkestra gives you consistent virtuosity with a signifying swerve. As we shall see, these guys aren't for real: they're for myth!

The second track, "Outer Spaceways, Inc." was my favorite at the time. Clocking in at a mere 1:05, it is a good example of Ra's "space chants." These are eminently hummable and singable ditties that the Arkestra began to record and include in their live shows as early as 1960 ("Interplanetary Music" and "We Travel the Spaceways"), quasi-pop songs with hooks. They have a way of sticking in your mind.

My attraction to the song was no coincidence. Sun Ra was first and foremost a teacher. Like Ralph Waldo Emerson, that other great American romantic pedagogue, Ra realized that you had to meet your audience on many levels and give them many things (advanced and elementary instruction); moreover, that it pays to restate complex teachings in simpler, varied forms. A typical Emerson address contained aphorisms and proverbs, poetry, straight exposition and philosophical explanation—often reiterating similar points about self-reliance or the Oversoul or fate in these various idioms. Similarly, a Ra concert or recording can include poetry, sermonizing, space chants, traditional jazz, "outside" (but not free) playing, dance, light-shows, film, and theater to reinforce his message in sundry media. (Don't worry; we'll address what that message might be below. As he wrote in a later song, "I'll wait for you.") He can attract most people on some level. Biographer and Ra scholar John Szwed explains:

> With Sun Ra, it was up to you to make sense of what he said, to find in it what you could use. You had to engage your spirit to understand him, but it was your spirit which was always in control, not Sun Ra. It was that attitude that audiences who responded to Sun Ra's music took to the performances. You accepted what you liked and ignored the too-far-out, the obscure or embarrassing parts. And he in turn ignored the Philistines in his audience. Or transvalued their comments. A teenager once said to him, "This is sixth-grade jazz!" "Yeah," he answered, "because the average American has a sixth-grade education, so thank you, I'm reaching them."
>
> "Sun Ra didn't say you had to believe what he says; you should just check it out for yourself," said Danny Thompson [baritone sax player and flautist for the Arkestra]. (385)

Ra, after all, was trained as a teacher at Alabama A & M in 1936, and would eventually give public lectures and teach a course at Berkeley. He knew how to communicate knowledge to people. As Ra said elsewhere, "A natural musician should 'move' all the people—whether they love him or not. It's like the rain, or the sun which shines in many different ways" (Carles).

On that second track, I got his message loud and clear:

> If you find Earth boring
> Just the same old same thing
> Come on sign up
> Come to Outer Spaceways, Inc.

How could I resist? He was offering to get me off the planet to explore the cosmos.

The next track, "Scene 1, Take 1," was a Moog synthesizer solo (possibly his very best ever) that veered from ethereal shimmering to gutbucket abrasiveness. But was it jazz? On the one hand, in name only because it was on a record best filed under jazz. On the other hand, as Thelonious Monk once said in defense of Ra as a jazz artist, "it swings" (Szwed 219-20).

The second side had more unusual sounds: "Pyramids," a spacemaster keyboard solo with drums in the background; "Interpretation," a brooding chamber piece for strange stringed instruments and a "space dimension mellophone" [a mellophone fitted with a mouthpiece for another instrument, perhaps a bassoon]; "Ancient Ethiopia," a big Cadillac arrangement of an older Ra composition highlighting drums and baritone saxophone; and finally "Strange Worlds," another alien soundscape with trumpet flares, James Jacson playing the ancient Egyptian infinity drum with his curved candy cane mallets, and the great vocals of June Tyson evoking "strange worlds" with her space ethnicities and distortions. A final blast of the space key and the needle went off the record. Amazing stuff! I had heard Sun Ra's "angels and demons at play," an intriguing mix of consonance (the angels) and dissonance (the demons). My ears stayed open.

After that, I was always on the alert for Sun Ra cutouts. The first few I acquired after *The Solar-Myth Approach, Volume 2* were pretty conservative for Ra. *Sun Song* and *Sound of Joy* were Delmark reissues of 1956 recordings that were much more "inside" than what I had previously heard (although avant-garde jazzer Anthony Braxton recommends "Brainville" off the former as one of two essential Ra compositions for study [in Corbett 217]). When I went to graduate school in North Carolina, I made happier discoveries on Franklin street in Chapel Hill at Schoolkids Records: a cut-out double album *Live at Montreux* (1976) which contained a vital mix of adventurous soloing, quintessential Ra compositions such as "Lights on a Satellite" and "El is the Sound of Joy," and a sublime cover of "Take the A Train" (Billy Strayhorn's signature composition for Duke Ellington). At Schoolkids, I also acquired my first really homemade El Saturn release, *Sound Mirror* (1978); it had minimal information on a piece of paper taped to the front of the otherwise blank record jacket. Eventually I would come to acquire a lot more of these from mail order (Rounder Records in Boston), Schoolkids and at live gigs.

For I became a hopeless Ra admirer in the late seventies when I first saw him in concert at D. C. Space (aptly named) in Washington, D. C.. If you have open eyes and ears, once you see the Arkestra you're hooked! When Sun Ra came out in his purple robes and stared into my eyes, I had no doubt of his sincerity or his genius. He projected a gentle seriousness, tempered by a hint of whimsy. In a word, his presence was regal even in that dingy punk club.

The show, of course, was fantastic—a veritable anthology of the black arts from Africa through Harlem to the space age. Saxophone players climbed up on our tables to blow us personal solos; dancers and players marched and chanted through the space of the nightclub. This version of the Arkestra was smaller than some of the more elaborate presentations which included fire-eaters and tumblers. But it was more spectacle than I had ever seen before or since in concert (except for the other four times I saw the Arkestra). Sun Ra knew how to mix it up with an audience and give them a tailor-made concert.

The music was wonderful as well, naturally. By then Ra had patented a mix of group improvisation, his own compositions, a standard or two and some closing space chants. During these the band would march offstage, wend through the audience, go backstage and return for the encore singing, playing and clapping all the while. I have since seen Moroccan bands in Marrakech execute these maneuvers, but such an approach is a rarity in these United States.

After seeing the cosmo-drama, the rest is history. I am grateful to a late friend, Greg Bovee, for taping four sets over two days at a Milwaukee jazz club in the early 1980s, and for helping me to obtain some of the rarer Saturn offerings. I don't have all of Sun Ra's recordings. (Does anyone? I doubt it.) But I have enough to share with you some highlights and give you something to look for in used record stores, at yard sales, or online.

But Is It Jazz?

One logical place to start considering the music of Sun Ra is to address the serious issue of its genre. Like Joni Mitchell, Ra was somewhat resistant to easy labeling and aware that he was doing something ultimately outside the categorical boxes listeners rely upon to process the shock of the new. (Think of how people hasten to read titles and accompanying text in art museums.) A closer examination of this music will frustrate any attempt to box it in.

The Arkestra emerged in the mid-fifties during the mass popularity of be-bop jazz and were naturally associated with that movement, especially by white jazz critics. Be-bop (later bop) was characterized by a freer relationship towards the melody and harmony of the source material than earlier eras of jazz attempted. The improviser could just cut to the chords of the song and play them forwards, backwards or sideways—a sonic breakthrough comparable to cubism in the visual arts. When coupled with driving rhythms ultimately derived from West African techniques, this was a frenetic music well-suited to the post-atomic age of anxiety. Too far out for some listeners, it attracted progressive audiences across ethnic lines and made careers (if not wealth) for players such as Charlie Parker, Dizzy Gillespie and Thelonious Monk. There is no doubting that individual members of the Arkestra thoroughly understood this music and could deploy its approaches: John Gilmore's work on tenor sax immediately comes to mind.

But, as critic Art Lange reminds us, be-bop "held no charms for Ra," whose roots and initial allegiances as an older man who arrived on Earth in 1914 were in the Swing Era (liner notes for *We Travel the Spaceways*). As is often documented, Sun Ra served an apprenticeship with the Fletcher Henderson orchestra after he moved from Birmingham to Chicago. Fletcher Henderson (1897-1952), one of the founders of swing, was based at the Club DeLisa, a south side juke joint and casino. In the late 1940s, Sun Ra (then technically Herman Poole Blount) took over as pianist and eventually co-arranger for the Club DeLisa's house bands, first Henderson and then later Red Saunders (Szwed 53-7). He received a fine training for a future band leader; the point of this narrative, however, is that Ra initially learned Swing Era, big band compositional approaches. Specifically, he acquired a taste for discipline—a touchstone throughout his career. Be-bop would have represented the opposite values for him: wildness, self-indulgence and indiscipline. Although the Arkestra produced far more adventurous music than the bop players throughout its career, there were always contexts and codes—even scores—constraining the expressive elements of the band.

There are plenty of be-bop moments in the Arkestra's long performance history, acknowledging its presence as a possible jazz idiom. For example, the trading of solos rapidly between players on a cover of Gershwin's "But Not For Me" is standard bop practice (on *Standards* [2001, but recorded 1962-3]). And John Gilmore's earlier solo work often resembles be-bop in technique (e.g., "Urnack" off *Angels and Demons at Play* [recorded in 1956, issued in 1965 (Szwed 177)]). But Sun Ra was expanding the Swing Era into the space age, first and foremost; be-bop was only a sideshow for him.

Generically, the same is even more evident in the case of the free jazz movement that began with Ornette Coleman and eventually flourished in the sixties and early seventies. Again, Sun Ra and his Arkestra seemed to embody its approach, and even anticipate it. Free jazz employed techniques like simultaneous soloing and an emphasis on conversationally improvised communication between players of a highly spontaneous and unrepeatable nature. It sounded like Ra was doing this from as early as the appropriately named track "The Beginning" from *The Futuristic Sounds of Sun Ra* (1961). And by 1965, he was clearly recording pieces with a strong family resemblance to free jazz, like "The Magic City" (off the eponymous recording)—which John Gilmore admitted was "unreproducible, a tapestry of sound" (Szwed 214).

Nonetheless, Ra always took care to dissociate himself from the movement. In a 1975 interview he joked:

> A lot of musicians have been trying to come to Philadelphia and stay with me ... . I say, "Stay where you are if you're one of the freedom boys, because I'm dealing with discipline." All men can get into the freedom thing, but I'm on the discipline plane. I tell my Arkestra that all humanity is in some kind of restricted limitation, but they're in the Ra jail, and it's the best jail in the world. (in Blumenthal)

More technically, he pointed out that "I can write you something so chaotic you would say you know it's not written. But the reason it's chaotic is because it's written to be. It's further out than anything they would be doing if they were just improvising" (liner notes, *When Angels Speak of Love* [2000]).

A simple test case you can make is to play side by side one of Ra's "freer" compositions with any straight-up example of free jazz. The trick nowadays can be getting ahold of a recording of the latter; much fell out of print. I conducted this experiment by juxtaposing "The Magic City" by Ra with Alan Silva's Celestrial Communication Orchestra's recording of "Seasons," a six-sided improvisation with some minimal scoring. This latter is an especially interesting case: not only was Alan Silva in the Arkestra, but he made this recording in Paris only a month after playing with Ra in West Berlin (his recording is from December 1970). Although "Seasons" is not without merit or interest (its main theme recalls the Mexican horror film "Braniac" music used by Zappa on *Bongo Fury*), it is palpably not as compositionally complex as the Ra composition—despite having six times the length! There is a great deal of noodling and self-indulgent blowing with no seeming direction. Sun Ra, by contrast, is always conducting and taking the listener along on a cognitive and emotional ride. The Arkestra has freedom, but it is always constrained by discipline—wild solo moments in a larger structure. This is more easily heard than described, and it may be a difference of degree rather than kind. Nonetheless, it is a serious misnomer to lump even Ra's most adventurous work in with free jazz.

But why quibble about be-bop and free jazz when Ra occasionally denied he was even really playing jazz? In the liner notes he wrote for *Jazz in Silhouette* (1958), he described his music as "THE SOUND OF SILHOUETTES IMAGES AND FORECASTS OF TOMORROW DISGUISED AS JAZZ" (block capitals are Ra's). In other words, jazz music itself was just a generic mask he wore for his actual purposes, something to file his music under for convenience.

Finally, although "some may recall him as one of the great avant-gardists of the second half of the twentieth century," Ra did not like that label either

(Szwed 382). John Szwed points out on this same page of his biography how Ra's music was too positive and inclusive to resemble the pessimism and nihilism of much of the avant-garde. But Ra says it best again: "[my music is] more than avant-garde, because the 'avant-garde' refers to, I suppose, advanced earth music, but this is not earth music. It has nothing to do with it. Music that's from a celestial plane, it's not a part of this planet" (Corbett 311).

For Sun Ra himself, this was space music when all was said and done—not jazz or avant-garde earth music (Szwed 141). He was trying to depict his mental (the safest position, I know) travels through the cosmos by means of sound. His co-partner in Saturn Research, Alton Abraham, gives some ultimate insight into how serious this all was for the inner circle when he talks of secret codes that produce the music belonging only to the Ra "frat," and when he assures interviewer Corbett that he, Alton Abraham, "can write the music, the space music" (225, 227). Alton Abraham attributes the change in John Coltrane's style after 1956 to Arkestra member Pat Patrick slipping him some of the codes (Corbett 225). If this all smacks of Pythagoreanism, Gnosticism and hermeticism, so be it. Ra ran not only one of the best jails in the world, but one of the most interesting ones. Let's investigate this space music disguised as jazz and the man who transcribed it, after laying one last generic issue to rest.

But Is It Avant-Pop?

By this point, you might be questioning why Sun Ra was in my book, *Adventures in Avant Pop*. If Yoko Ono and Frank Zappa tended towards the avant-garde end of avant-pop, and Neil Young and Joni Mitchell towards the pop end, Ra seems off the charts altogether—literally. I have already mentioned how Radio Pacifica gave him rare airplay only after he died; none of his records ever graced the Billboard charts. Ken Burns neglected to mention him even once in his mammoth *Jazz* documentary (which did take time to name-check musicians influenced by Ra such as the Art Ensemble of Chicago). We have already seen Ra's problematizing of his avant-garde status; what on earth makes him a pop musician?

I will submit that it is a matter of intention rather than necessarily achievement. If Ra never charted, it wasn't for his lack of trying. Unlike avant-garde musicians such as Anthony Braxton or John Cage, Ra and his Arkestra repeatedly reached out to the masses—albeit unsuccessfully by industry standards. I have already suggested, for starters, that Ra was a consummate showman. The Arkestra always gave its public top value on their entertainment dollar. No wonder promoter and activist John Sinclair described his double bill of Sun Ra and the Arkestra opening for James

Brown at the 1974 Ann Arbor Blues and Jazz Festival (in exile in Windsor, Ontario) as the "Dream Show of All Time" (liner notes, *It Is Forbidden*, capitals Sinclair's). The aforementioned space chants sung in the show especially gestured towards the most accessible kinds of popular music.

Aside from Ra's popular outreach as a performer, which won him fans at rock festivals as well as jazz gatherings, he took part in many commercial projects without any elitist condescension. In fact, Sun Ra's first recorded work (under the name of Herman "Sonny" Blount) was playing barrelhouse piano for the lewd blues shouter Wynonie Harris. (One of another connections between Ra and James Brown is that Brown initially went for a vocal delivery like that of Harris [Smith 56]). The four songs, singles on Nashville's Bullet label that required Ra to travel from his Chicago home base in 1946, were double-entendre blues and boogie (the word itself a double entendre!). Sun Ra would seldom revert to this style of playing with his own band, but it is telling if not surprising that he could readily work in such an idiom thoroughly associated with "race" records. Ra's most energetic playing is on "Dig This Boogie." The other tracks are of more interest perhaps for Harris' lyrics, which are not like anything else in the Ra catalogue of originals or covers. "Lightnin' Struck the Poorhouse" seems to be about white lightning moonshine bankrupting the singer who hasn't "got a dime" after the meteorological event. "Drinkin' By Myself" (because he's "feelin' low down and lonesome") contains a blues trope that becomes almost ubiquitous after Fats Domino: "You never miss your water / Till your well runs dry."

In addition, Ra released many 45 rpm singles throughout his career—enough to more than fill a double CD compilation on the Evidence label. Ra began working with doo-wop groups like The Nu Sounds and The Cosmic Rays in Chicago during the mid-fifties.[1] A casual listen to the CD will tell you these are pure pop songs, only hinting at Ra's metaphysical interests:

> If you live in fables
> Then you'll know what I mean
> For that is a world
> Where things aren't what they seem ("Dreaming," The Cosmic
>   Rays [1956])

Sun Ra released many other such pop projects on his Saturn label, including holiday songs that he co-wrote with Alton Abraham ("Happy New Year To You!" and "It's Christmas Time" with The Qualities [1956]; Ra also played harmonium on the tracks [liner notes, *The Singles*]). Or how about his piano work on the Saturn single "Teenager's Letter of Promises" (Juanita Rogers and Lynn Hollings with Mr. V's Five Joys [1958 or 1959])? Is that pop enough for you? I don't think there's anything like that lurking in the John Cage catalogue.

Other more commercial single releases include several with a character named Yochanan, a vocal wild man cut from the same cloth as Screaming Jay Hawkins. In addition to gutbucket race records like "Muck Muck" and "Hot Skillet Mama" (both 1957), Yochanan had his own extraterrestrial rap down claiming to be "The Sun Man" on several tunes (1959 or 1960). The Arkestra and Sun Ra accompanied him on all these ventures (liner notes, *The Singles*).

Sun Ra and the Arkestra themselves released at least two potential chart-toppers. "I'm Gonna Unmask The Batman" was a novelty release hampered undoubtedly by its infelicitous 1974 issuance between the Batman television series and the character's pop culture revival courtesy of Frank Miller's *Dark Knight* graphic novel and Tim Burton's films. Its flipside, "The Perfect Man," was pure synthesizer pop music in the same ballpark as other seventies products like Emerson, Lake & Palmer.

In 1965, Ra played piano and harpsichord for jazz vibist Walt Dickerson on an unusual outing entitled *Impressions of a Patch of Blue*. This was a series of jazz extensions of the Jerry Goldsmith instrumental music for the Sidney Poitier film of the same name. Although the interplay was lovely (Ra would work intermittently with Dickerson over the years), the project was doomed because of the marginal interest the public had in the original film score. Who cares about a jazz interpretation of pop melodies that aren't popular? Francis Davis admits in his witty liner notes on the reissue that the album "was aiming for the sort of casual record buyer who thinks he likes jazz but prefers hearing songs with which he is already at least vaguely familiar." This target audience was never reached, but a great album of chamber jazz was produced.

The Arkestra's own album releases delve less frequently into gestures towards the mass market, but there are stellar exceptions. Most oddly, there is the much better timed (but nonetheless not terribly successful) 1966 *Batman and Robin* record marketed for children. On this gig, the Arkestra played with members of the Blues Project rock band (including Al Kooper joining Ra on organ). This amalgam was called for little apparent reason other than its catchiness "The Sensational Guitars of Dan and Dale." Although Danny Kalb was one of the guitarists there was no Dale. The music is pretty much what you'd expect: cheesy sixties instrumental music. There are some good musical jokes, however. Ra sneaks in a Tchaikovsky quote on his organ during "Penguin's Umbrella"; "Batmobile Wheels" recycles the melody from the pop hit "A Groovy Kind of Love" (itself based on a Clementi *sonatina*). There's also some respectable playing from Gilmore's gutbucket tenor on "The Bat Cave" and the whole ensemble grooves at length on "Batman and Robin Over the Rooftops."

Then there was Sun Ra's disco phase in the late seventies! Like Frank

Zappa and James Brown (and even Yoko Ono if you consider "Walking on Thin Ice" as a club track, which it was), Sun Ra saw musical opportunities in the disco craze. He made his band members listen to examples of the genre. When they told him it was "hokey shit," he responded that "[t]his hokey shit is somebody's hopes and dreams ... . Don't be so hip!" (Szwed 352). Ra made a series of records that attempted to please these listeners, beginning with the drum machine and keyboard groove of "Constellation" (1978, issued on both *Other Voices, Other Blues* and *Media Dream*). Pre-programmed keyboard sound loops and drum machines accompanied Ra's organ work and various horn and reed players on a series of late seventies recordings: "Disco 3000," "Dance of the Cosmo-Aliens" (both off *Disco 3000* [1978], the former was also issued as the edited single "Disco 2100") and "UFO" (off *On Jupiter* [1979]).

There is no evidence to suggest the disco community embraced these rather eccentric efforts, too complex to be really danceable. John Szwed honestly and charitably labels them "revisionist disco" (350). As some of the titles indicate, one could also think of them as a kind of science-fiction projection of what disco might sound like had it continued to be musically dominant—a quaint sonic equivalent to the Futurama exhibit at the 1939 New York World's Fair, an alternate tomorrow.

I am puzzled as to why Szwed refers to *Lanquidity* (1978) as also revisionist disco, however. Now that Evidence has reissued this rare recording, one can see it was a serious bid for a larger audience. But its popular genre is not so much disco as smooth or mellow jazz of a sort produced at the time by the likes of Eddie Harris, Grover Washington, Jr., and Stanley Turrentine. Certainly Sun Ra's most accessible album, it has a late-night urban feel reflecting the circumstances of its recording: an all-night session in New York at a professional studio (Buchler, liner notes). Only the surreal whisper-chants of "There Are Other Worlds (They Have Not Told You Of)" break the trance induction of the rest of the album ("They want to speak to you"). The lineup of the Arkestra was very full and strong for this session: John Gilmore on tenor, Marshall Allen on oboe and alto, James Jacson on bassoon, relative newcomer Michael Ray on trumpet, several hot guitarists—to name only a few players and instruments. As a result, *Lanquidity* manages to be both of its time and genre and fresh (unlike most seventies smooth jazz, which sounds like a soundtrack for a coke binge!). The players made all the difference here; they're making a pop record, but they hint of other worlds. Musical ones as well as physical ones ... .

In the early eighties, the sixty-eight year old Ra recorded a timely "protest rap" (Szwed 353) with "Nuclear War" (on the eponymous release and *A Fireside Chat with Lucifer*). Released in 1982, the same year as Grandmaster Flash's "The Message" and well before Public Enemy, "Nuclear War" skewers the militaristic pretensions of winnable nuclear war originally espoused by the Reagan administration:

> It's a motherfucker
> Don't you know
> If they push that button
> Your ass got to go

From my admittedly biased perspective, I think this is Ra and the Arkestra's wittiest moment among many. He was caught in a catch-22: to really tell it like it was, he had to transcend FCC regulations. It should have been a monster hit, and was indeed covered by some rock musicians (Brian Ritchie of the Violent Femmes and Yo La Tengo [in four separate readings; see below]).

Sun Ra's last massive pop gesture began when the Arkestra was asked to contribute a song to *Stay Awake*, a 1988 tribute to the film music of Walt Disney. The band performed "Pink Elephants on Parade" from *Dumbo* with zany brio. Perhaps responding to Disney's discipline and technological innovation, as well as the ubiquity of this music in our culture, Ra embraced him as a genius on a par with Fletcher Henderson and Duke Ellington. Renaming the Arkestra (a band with many thematic sub-names over the years) as the Disney Odyssey Arkestra, he toured in 1989 with a largely Disney program to "show the cosmic forces that there have been some people who came this way who were very nice ... . [I]t's a shield of beauty" (Szwed 361-2). I've always wondered whether he noticed or cared about Disney's racist moments (the crows in *Dumbo* come to mind), or whether he simply transcended such issues from his extraterrestrial perspective. In any event, the Arkestra took back Disney songs like "Zip-A-Dee-Doo-Dah" (from the essentially suppressed *Song of the South*) more dramatically than U2 did "Helter Skelter" on *Rattle and Hum*. It's a rare treat to hear these Arkestra covers on *Second Star to the Right (Salute to Walt Disney)* (1989). John Szwed beat me to the punch in observing that "The Forest of No Return" (from *Babes in Toyland*) sounds like it already was a Ra composition (362)! This live compilation could also work as a children's record.

Even after Ra's passing, the ghost band Arkestra continued to perform Disney material. In the late nineties, I saw the band cover the Mickey Mouse Club Theme, replete with a dancer dressed like Minnie Mouse and audience participation, as well as "Zip-A-Dee-Doo-Dah." It was real, it was natural: everything was satisfactual!

Throughout its career, Sun Ra's Arkestra made gestures of popular outreach not only to children and trend-following young adults, but also to older generations. Consider how many standards the Arkestra played through the years, always reverentially in intention even if the execution might have been unusual: "I Could Have Danced All Night" (*Sound Sun Pleasure!!*, 1958), "Autumn in New York" (*What's New?*, 1962), "Nature Boy" (*Some Blues But Not the Kind That's Blue*, 1977), "Smile" (*Celestial Love*, 1982) or "Days of Wine and Roses" (*Live at Praxis '84 Volume III*), to name but a few. In addition to show tunes and pop ballads, the Arkestra also repeatedly covered the standards of the jazz canon (Ellington and Strayhorn, Fletcher Henderson, Thelonious Monk). Any demographic which braved the concerts would have found something tailored for its tastes.

A final popular dimension of Sun Ra worth noting is his 1974 film *Space Is the Place*. Although it remained sub-underground in distribution until its 1993 release on video (from Rhapsody Films), it was a fine contribution to the popular blaxploitation genre. The film is only 63 minutes in length because Ra vetoed the sex scenes that were otherwise typical for this popular genre (Szwed 332). What remains is a mythic tale of Sun Ra playing for "the end of the world" with a mysterious adversary called "The Overseer." Ra flies a spaceship that runs on music and has various encounters with the residents of seventies Oakland. Its most memorable line is his threat to teenage girls who don't want to go to outer space with him that he might just "chain [them] up, take [them] with [him]" like their ancestors. Like Neil Young's *Human Highway*, there is a suitably apocalyptic ending to this funky rewrite of *The Seventh Seal*. *Space Is the Place* was certainly populist in intent, if not popular in box office take: Sun Ra's imaginative bid for a black space program.

Where Is Sun Ra Coming From, Besides Saturn?

John Szwed begins his biography of Sun Ra with a 1954 quote from Louis Armstrong: "Our music is a Secret Order" (vii). Along with the previously mentioned remarks of Alton Abraham, this comment reminds us that there has always been a hermetic element to the jazz tradition—one which Ken Burns was certainly not given access to as an outsider when he made his documentary, which accounts for its superficial coverage. I'm not claiming I have much contact with it either, being an extreme amateur as a musician. But I know folks who do! On the most mysterious level, jazz has its "codes," which Abraham claimed he, Ra and some Arkestra veterans possessed. Perhaps these are no more than the space-age versions of Frank Zappa's remark that accomplished musicians know how to manipulate the emotions of their listeners. Or an extreme version of the obvious ways jazz technique is passed on: tutoring worthy disciples, humiliating rivals in all-night "cutting contests," wood-shedding in private after being exposed to new ideas (sometimes for years).

Sun Ra repeatedly admitted that his earthly hometown of Birmingham,

Alabama, exposed him to all the music he would ever need to hear in the form of largely undocumented African-American touring big bands such as the Carolina Cotton Pickers. (You can hear one recording of theirs on Spotify: "Western [Moten] Swing."). As Sun Ra reveals,

> I never missed a band, whether a known or unknown unit. I loved music beyond the state of liking it. Some of the bands I heard never got popular and never made hit records, but they were truly natural black beauty. I want to thank them, and I will give honor to all the sincere musicians who ever were or ever will be. It's wonderful to even think about such people. The music they played was a natural happiness of love, so rare I cannot explain it. It was fresh and courageous, daring, sincere, unfettered. It was unmanufactured avant-garde, and still is, because there was no place for it in the world; so the world neglected something of value and did not understand. And all along I could not understand why the world did not understand.
>
> What happened is that, in the Deep South, the black people were very oppressed and were made to feel like they weren't anything, so the only thing they had was big bands. Unity showed that the black man could join together and dress nicely, do something nice, and that was all they had ... . So it was important for us to hear big bands. (Szwed 16-7)

Anyone who listens to the Arkestra will hear this tradition preserved, if transformed—which is what any jazz player inevitably does to the tradition. But Ra concedes the origins of his music are but a memory, for reasons as diverse as racism, economics and technological limitation. The earliest roots on record readily available to the genealogically inclined would be the swing records of Fletcher Henderson, which young Herman Blount had listened to for years before he moved to Chicago and actually played with Henderson's band (Szwed 11).

What does one hear on these records that became Ra's? A tough question, because most of Henderson's contributions to the idiom can be found elsewhere. Big band swing is an over-determined text: who can say for sure who contributed what? (A problem that extends, of course, to all music.) What matters most is not whether Fletcher Henderson did something first, but that Sun Ra heard it very early on.

Fletcher Henderson is credited in the jazz histories with the incorporation of the innovations of Louis Armstrong into the larger jazz ensemble, a development that turned jazz into swing (Schuller 1-2). What Louis Armstrong did was to develop a playful relationship to melody and rhythm: you could bend the notes of the song, or sustain them, or omit them altogether.

(Listen to "Potato Head Blues," for example.) Sun Ra has commented on the importance of this approach:

> You should play it wrong—a little ahead of the beat. That's the way the older jazz musicians played it. They played it a little ahead, then later, Chicago musicians decided to play a bit behind the beat and that's not easy to do. It's a little ahead or behind. Then there's music that's right on the beat. Well, white people can do that. If it's on the beat they got you, and say, "That's my stuff!" If you get ahead of the beat or behind the beat they be talking about you and say it ain't even music, 'cause they can't play it. If you can play on the beat you can forget it, you won't have a job. So stay ahead of the beat, something you can't count. (Szwed 99-100)

Fletcher Henderson got his band to do this, emulating what he heard from Louis Armstrong himself when he was in the Henderson orchestra. At first only a few soloists, like Coleman Hawkins on tenor sax, could pull it off. But by the thirties, Henderson's entire band could swing.

Other innovations accomplished by Fletcher Henderson included composing for the orchestra sectionally (like classical musicians had been doing, but unlike earlier jazz practice). The reeds would be doing one thing, the trumpets another, the percussion section would be laying down a different rhythm than the rest (Schuller 2). Often this would be refined into a call-and-response effect, with one section answering another like the African-American congregation responding to the exhortations of the preacher. (Check out Henderson compositions such as "The Stampede," "Copenhagen" or "King Porter Stomp" [this last covered by the Arkestra] to hear this in practice.) The Arkestra's careful mixture of composed material and solo improvisation is an elaboration of the Henderson approach heard as early as "Copenhagen" (recorded in 1924). The insanely tight and fast reed section work on a Ra composition such as "The Shadow World" seems to be pushing the innovative approach of Henderson to a kind of sublime *reductio ad absurdum*.

Other elements that arguably passed from Henderson's practice to Ra's were the former's love of lush "Cadillac" arrangements (e.g., "Wrappin' It Up") and even occasional tendencies towards exotic and / or orientalist scene-painting ("The Gouge of Armour Avenue," "Shanghai Shuffle"). You can hear exfoliations of Henderson's Cadillac approach on Ra compositions such as "Saturn" or "Lights on a Satellite." As for Ra's scene-painting, it extends from the local (Birmingham ["The Magic City"], Chicago ["El is a Sound of Joy"], New York ["Manhattan Cocktail"]) through the terrestrial exotic ("Overtones of China," "Ancient Ethiopia") to the vast universe itself ("Friendly Galaxy," "Strange Worlds"). Duke Ellington also had these elements in his work, of course; but Henderson was doing it first. Sun Ra's writing seems to be an extension of both into the space age.

Along with the great African-American swing tradition, Sun Ra also seemed to be aware of a fifties trend in Euro-American music: the high-fidelity lounge exotica of composers and performers such as Les Baxter and Martin Denny (Szwed 151). After its initial popularity in the 1950s, this was a neglected music until *Re/Search* magazine put out its *Incredibly Strange Music* issues and CDs in the early nineties. Exotica, and the lounge genre it was a subset of, were buried by rock and roll before the fairly recent lounge revival. Its initial popularity was a result of a concatenation of circumstances: American exposure to Oceanic culture as a result of the second World War's Pacific theater, which culminated in the statehood of Hawaii; the boom in audio-electronic innovations, which led to a craze for high-fidelity and stereo experimentation; the conspicuous consumption of the Eisenhower populuxe era, which caused a boom in cocktail, space-age and / or tiki paraphernalia. After all, this last juxtaposition became the caucasoid version of Sun Ra's juxtaposition of outer space and ancient Egypt (co-opted by the *Stargate* film and its televisual spinoffs). If you find the right bar on Cocoa Beach, Florida, you can see simultaneously a fake Easter Island head and the launch pad for the space shuttle! I've done it. Future primitive was in, and still leaves its traces on the space coast.[2]

Sun Ra certainly picked up on many elements of this music, and it helps give the Arkestra its uncanny ambience: it's the added ingredient outside the main tradition of the jazz big band, although the exotica of Henderson and Ellington are a plausible influence upon Les Baxter and Martin Denny. Les Baxter is an especially crucial link here. Like Ra, he was interested from the beginning in electronic instruments. Baxter pioneered the theremin synthesizer on *Music Out of the Moon* (1947), a year before Ra may have recorded "Deep Purple" (with Stuff Smith) playing his Solovox.

Some Arkestra selections pay deep homage to this music. Consider, for example, the hypnotic drumming and processionals of "Watusa" (or "Watusi," depending upon the recording: they are slightly different pieces sometimes but other times it's just an interchangeable name) or "Africa"—both off *Lady with the Golden Stockings* (recorded 1959, issued 1966, reissued 1967 as *The Nubians of Plutonia* [Szwed 171, 429]). Sun Ra could have almost made it as a lounge act, in fact; his only problem was that his music was often too intense to be truly ambient background for bachelor pads. In Brian Eno's famous formulation of the criterion for ambient music, Ra's music was not "as ignorable as it is listenable" (liner notes, *Music for Airports*). The Arkestra has a way of waking you up, unlike Denny or most of Baxter (whose emotional sonic experiment, *The Passions* [1954], is a telling exception: check out "Terror," for example).

Big band swing and hi-fi exotica, when combined and extended with post-bop innovations in playing technique, offer a plausible lineage for the sounds of Sun Ra and his Arkestra. But that's only half the story, of course: the Arkestra is a marching (literally) encyclopedia of black performance and spectacle. The roots for these elements go as far back as Herman Blount's exposure to precision marching at age ten as a member of the American Woodmen Junior Division, a Euro-American philanthropy for African-Americans comparable to the Boy Scouts (Szwed 9-10). The travelling big bands undoubtedly also showed performance tricks and techniques to an admiring youngster. All these elements entered into the mix of the Arkestra's development. By the time they held down Slug's tavern Monday nights in mid-sixties New York, all the elements of the Arkestra show were in place. As Szwed says:

> They were reasserting black performance values which were completely alien to white experience, conventions drawn from the church, the black cabaret, bar life, and the community picnic; they were reclaiming the aesthetics of those Amiri Baraka called the Blues People: honking and shrieking saxophones, bar walking, guitar playing behind the head, eccentric dancers, capes and exotic costumes, weeping and pleading on bended knees, ecstatic states of speech and dance—the flash of the show, the elements which James Brown and Jimi Hendrix were startling whites with elsewhere: "They didn't know how to take us," [James] Jacson said. "As a bunch of drunks? Some slightly crazy people? A bunch of addicts? But whatever we were, they knew we were not broken men." (227-8)

Such were the main ingredients in the cosmo-drama's sound and look. But there were conceptual elements in it as well.

Was Sun Ra From Saturn?

As John Szwed ruefully acknowledges, much of the white critical discourse around Sun Ra inevitably genuflects at this tedious honky shrine: was Sun Ra a "genius," a "charlatan" or a "madman" (xvii)? Look at all the liner notes written by white critics for his various albums and CDs. However much they may admire Ra and his music, they feel compelled to bring this question up—even if only to dismiss it. They protest too much. Like those first concertgoers at Slug's, they still don't know how to take Ra, really.

I'd like to sidestep this minimally interesting question and address the far more compelling consideration of Ra's beliefs. James Jacson hits the nail on the head in the above quote when he asserts "they knew we were not broken men." Sun Ra's insistence that "[he] never felt like [he] was part of this planet" was an empowering one for him: as June Tyson would sing in the Arkestra, Ra became "the living myth" (Szwed 6).

I have an odd perspective on all this, because as a middle-schooler I briefly claimed I was from another planet! I parlayed somatic tricks such as the hereditary ability to make the pupils of my eyes vibrate, and some rhetorical skills, to maintain this ruse—frankly, as a gambit to get attractive lasses intrigued with me. Such a stratagem was compensation for my blue-collar origins and uncouth appearance. As we shall see, James Brown likewise compensated for his own hardscrabble origins by turning himself into a living myth; Elvis did the same. My own foray into self-mythology was briefer, because my circumstances were better than these other folks'. But for James Brown, Elvis Presley and especially Sun Ra, the persona was sustained seamlessly in public for much longer. Though Brown and Presley occasionally slipped, no one ever saw Ra drop the mask in a moment of fatigue—or at least no one ever reported seeing such a thing. He was the Man from Saturn 24/7. What do you call a persona that you adopt around the clock? An identity, I would think. Sun Ra was the only version of Herman Blount we were ever going to get to know. Only the squares were bothered by that; the rest of us got with the program and acknowledged the living myth. It was the only game in town—or more accurately, in the omniverse!

Although I shall return to Ra's sense of alienation (literally being an alien!) from his arrival in Birmingham, Alabama, a clear watershed moment in Ra's self-formulation was his narration of alien abduction in the late nineteen thirties. This foundational account is worth quoting at length:

> ...[T]hese space men contacted me. They wanted me to go to outer space with them. They were looking for somebody who had that type of mind. They said it was quite dangerous because you had to have perfect discipline ... . I'd have to go up with no parts of my body touching outside of the beam, because if I did, going through different time zones, I wouldn't be able to get that far back. So that's what I did. And it's like, well, it looked like a giant spotlight shining down on me, and I call it transmolecularization, my whole body was changed into something else. I could see through myself. And I went up. Now, I call that an energy transformation because I wasn't in human form. I thought I was there, but I could see through myself.
>
> Then I landed on a planet that I identified as Saturn. First thing I saw was something like a rail, a long rail of railroad track coming out of the sky, and landed over there in a vacant lot ...

. Then I found myself in a huge stadium, and I was sitting in the last row, in the dark. I knew I was alone. They were down there, on the stage, something like a big boxing ring. So then they called my name, and I didn't move. They called my name again, and I still didn't answer. Then all at once they teleported me, and I was down there on that stage with them. They wanted to talk with me. They had one little antenna on each ear. A little antenna over each eye. They talked to me. They told me to stop [teachers' training] because there was going to be great trouble in schools. There was going to be trouble in every part of life. That's why they wanted to talk to me about it. "Don't have anything to do with it. Don't continue." They would teach me some things that when it looked like the world was going into complete chaos, when there was no hope for nothing, then I could speak, but not until then. I would speak, and the world would listen. That's what they told me.

Next thing, I found myself back on planet Earth in a room with them, and it was the back room of an apartment, and there was a courtyard. They was all with me. At the time, I wasn't wearing robes. I had on one of theirs, they put on me. They said, "Go out there and speak to them." And I looked out through the curtain and people were milling around in the courtyard. And I said, "No, they look like they're angry. I'm not going out there." So they pushed me through the curtain, and I found myself on a balcony, people milling around in the courtyard. They said, "They aren't angry, they're bewildered."

All of a sudden, the people were turning around, looking up to me on the balcony. (I was living in Chicago at that time.) I saw that I was laying down on a park bench, a stone park bench, in some park, near a river. There was a bridge. I knew it was New York City. I had done very well in Chicago and I thought that was one thing that could not happen. I looked and saw the sky was purple and dark red, and through that I could see the spaceships, thousands of them. And I sat up to look, then I heard a voice [say] "You can order us to land. Are conditions right for landing?" I think I said yes. They started to land, and there were people running to come to the landing, and they shot something like bullets. But they weren't bullets. They were something that when they hit the ground they were like chewing gum. It stuck people to the ground.

I came out of that. But [later] when I got to New York City, I was up near Columbia University. I saw the bench, I saw the bridge, so those things have been indelibly printed on my brain. I couldn't get them out if I tried. (in Szwed 29-30)

Both true believers in aliens and UFOs such as Whitley Streiber—as well as more skeptical analysts of UFO lore—have noted how UFO narratives like Ra's take on the coloration of the historical era in which they are experienced and recounted. From the Biblical claims of fiery wheels spinning in the air through the lore on goblins and fairies to the modern "grey" aliens in flying saucers, the variations of the tales produce a subject / object problem in accounting for the discrepancies. For example, John Keel posits thusly:

> That unidentified flying objects have been present since the dawn of man is an undeniable fact. They are not only described repeatedly in the Bible, but were also the subject of cave paintings made thousands of years before the Bible was written. And a strange procession of weird entities and frightening creatures have been with us just as long. When you review the ancient references you are obliged to conclude that the presence of these objects and beings *is a normal condition for this planet.* These things, these other intelligences ... either reside here but somehow remain concealed from us, or they do not exist at all and are actually special aberrations of the human mind— ... hallucinations, psychological constructs, momentary materializations of energy from that dimension beyond the reach of our senses and even beyond the reaches of our scientific instruments. They are not from outer space. There is no need for them to be. They have always been here. (15, italics Keel's)

This speculation might strike the casual reader as wilder than Ra's claims, but Keel gives himself several empiricist escape clauses courtesy of abnormal psychology. I appreciate, however, that Keel makes room for these encounters betokening some kind of reality—if not necessarily the one claimed by the informant. For Ra's account is a creakily anachronistic one: its tales of interplanetary monorails and chewing gum weapons align it solidly with science fiction writers such as A. E. Van Vogt and Cordwainer Smith, as well as fifties alien contactees like George Adamski. It has E. H. Gombrich's "invisible style" of its historical moment. So do Gilgamesh and the Book of Ezekiel. This is not to debunk, but to acknowledge the subject / object blurring in these mysterious accounts. The archetypal tale must pass though its particular teller. As for its ontological status, we could pick up Julian Jaynes' *The Origin of Consciousness in the Breakdown of the Bicameral Mind* and say that it's a mental phenomenon that we are hardwired for; or we could believe that other entities are surreptitiously co-inhabiting our world. John Keel's most subversive insinuation is that it really doesn't matter which option we pick: either way something odd is going on. Sun Ra clearly leaned towards the latter explanation, but we needn't if we don't want to—and we can still respect his account.

As Szwed notes, this narrative also resembles "a conversion experience and a call to preach in the Afro-Baptist tradition" (31). From this epiphany, it all proceeded: Ra's cosmo-doctrines, the music, the costumes, the drama. Sun Ra was a teacher first and foremost. It never got as much in the way of his art as it did for poet Ezra Pound, but these two men shared a certain obsessive dedication to their respective projects—as well as associational habits of mind divergent enough from conventional modes of thinking to inspire accusations of insanity from the skeptical. I cannot hope to convey to the general reader the full scope of Ra's beliefs and doctrines (which shifted over time in any case), but I can at least reference some of his most recurrent observations and assumptions.

Most of Ra's beliefs have pedigrees in world religious and philosophical thought; they result from his voluminous reading with Alton Abraham in Chicago. For example, consider his central doctrine on birth and death:

> ...[I]t is important to liberate oneself from the obligation to be born, because this experience doesn't help us at all. It is important for the planet that its inhabitants do not believe in being born, because whoever is born has to die. (Szwed 6)

For Sun Ra, life and being were opposed values to the cycle of birth and death, where death always and inevitably triumphs (as he joked in "The Possibility of Altered Destiny" lecture, "Die" is the one commandment of the creator we haven't been able to break yet!). Ra believed that you could transcend this mortal cycle through attaining access to a more spiritual plane through discipline and, yes, music. He would ask audience members to "give up [their] death" for him and travel the spaceways. Otherwise, the unenlightened are trapped on and in a world of death.

This belief obviously resembles many doctrines in world religion, ranging from all forms of Platonism and Gnosticism to Hindu and Buddhist doctrines of reincarnation and satori. The importance of music for the task recalls the doctrines of Pythagoras; the emphasis on discipline for transcendence reminds one of the teachings of Gurdjieff and Ouspensky. Ra had read all of these people, in fact, as Szwed's biography and Ra in interview demonstrate. His teachings were a syncretistic synthesis of what he liked about each set of beliefs—a mix-and-match approach to philosophy and religion reminiscent of his predecessor Emerson.

Sun Ra's dismissal of Christianity was no doubt abetted by his exposure to and interest in the German philosopher Nietzsche (Corbett 221). Ra was most hung up on the significance of the crucifixion:

> ... [W]hatever they're doing ends up in the graveyard. Even the Son of God ended up in the graveyard. Now, how could they teach a limited philosophy or a limited position like that...?
>
> ... He came and went right to the cross and said, "This is what God wants you to do: follow me." Ever since then they've been dying. If the Son of God died, well, God didn't save His own son; how can anybody think He's gonna save anybody else? His Son had to buy death; so will everybody else. He just came and showed them the way ... the way not to go. (Szwed 303)

Using his semantic equations, Ra would proceed to link the cross with the letter "X," the cruciform, the Roman numeral for ten. "Ten" reversed is "net," which he linked with Christ's injunction to his disciples to be "fishers of men" (Matthew 4:19; Szwed 303). Ergo, for Ra the cross was a net to snare men into the path of death.

The manner in which Ra argues involves etymological investigation and punning. He believed that God hid the truth after the fall of the Tower of Babel by using "phonetics" to hide true meanings in the great codes of world language and the Bible (in Meltzer 247). The undoing of post-Babel chaos and confusion occurs by means of a playful attention to counter-meanings revealed by etymology, wordplay and palindromic reversal. As the "X / ten / net" progression shows, Ra had no problem hopping from one language to another to follow a lead.

Ra's project has resonances with the linguistic experimentations and procedures of such luminaries as James Joyce, Jacques Derrida and John Cage. Like these gentlemen's efforts, his demonstrations of the fluidity of thought and language are both highly playful and imposing. For one thing, Ra was the master linguistic sorcerer: he would not be amused when band members he was instructing attempted these procedures themselves (Szwed 98). His thought processes were highly spontaneous and improvisatory in the spirit of jazz. But he assumed only a true leader of men could deploy his subversive approach—whence the importance of his foundational vision / calling. Such a stance seems highly plausible for an intelligent and creative autodidact. Behind all the wit and bluster, there must have been some lingering insecurities masked by the rigorous disciplining of his musicians.

And indeed, as Ra's take on Christianity shows, there is ample cause for doubt. Ra's obsession with the crucifixion leads him to neglect the resurrection part of the Gospel narrative! Ironically, his own *contemptus mundi* neoplatonic stance seems very harmonious with Christian doctrine. But his concentration on the sacrifice of the Son by the Father—itself plausibly defended as heralding an end to the sacrificial order by Rene Girard in *Things Hidden Since the Beginning of Time*—blinds Sun Ra to other aspects of Christian doctrine he might find more congenial to his own formulations.

My purpose here is to explicate Ra's beliefs rather than to defend or attack them, but this seems as good a moment as any to say *caveat emptor*. There are lots of interesting nuggets of insight scattered in Ra's works, but also all the deficiencies and cul-de-sacs of the street intellectual. Danny Thompson's advice to "just check it out for yourself" is again germane. Sooner or later everyone except Ra disagrees with Ra; if you don't, you're just not paying attention!

With this warning given, let's return to more of Sun Ra's especially recurrent claims. He also believed that Earth was inhabited by disguised angels and demons that interact among us. Again, this is a doctrine with a rich pedigree. The teachings of Emmanuel Swedenborg come to mind immediately. Swedenborg also believed in this concealed celestial conflict; Ra seems to have additionally absorbed the Swedish mystic's doctrine that "it's after the end of the world" (from the album of the same name). Both Ra and the Church of the New Jerusalem believe the last judgment has already occurred: we're just living out a kind of cosmic endgame! I raise this more obscure second point only as proof that Ra was very familiar with Swedenborgian doctrine and unafraid of incorporating it into his own doctrinal mosaic.

Ra's interest in the hidden angels and demons manifested in album titles (*Angels and Demons at Play*), song titles ("A Call for All Demons," "Demon's Lullaby") and the lyrics of space chants ("I know that I'm a member of the angel race / My home is over there in outer space" ["Angel Race," *Live from Soundscape* and elsewhere]). In a 1984 article in *Semiotexte*, Ra unpacked this belief at greatest length:

> You have to realize this planet is not only inhabited by humans, it's inhabited by aliens too. They got the books say they fell from heaven with Satan. So, in mixed up among humans you have angels. The danger spot is the United States. You have more angels in the country than anywhere else. You see, it was planned.
>
> I'll tell you something fantastic. It's unbelievable. They say that truth is stranger than fiction. Never in this history of the world has there been a case where you take a whole people and bring 'em into the country in the Commerce Department. Never before has that happened. It happened here. They bringing 'em in through the Commerce Department. It was possible for aliens and angels and devils and demons to come in this country. They didn't need no passport. So then they'd come in as displaced people. Perfect setup. So they come right on into the United States. They could come here and act like poor people, they could come here and act like slaves because they didn't keep up

with what was happening. They just brought some people in ... and said Oh you, they is nothing, they beastly. They brought 'em in here and doin' that, they allowed anything to come here. (in Meltzer 246-7)

Perhaps it is easier to grapple with this narrative as parable or myth rather than literal truth revealed by Ra. After all, his suggestion that angels, demons and aliens would have been caught by immigration if they hadn't gone through the Commerce Department seems unlikely at best. More likely, this tale is about the African-American paradox. Sun Ra early on realized that the skin game of being black in America was one he couldn't win, so he changed the rules and repatriated himself as a Saturnian.[3] The narrative above attempts to help other African-Americans by dialectically juxtaposing a myth of self-empowerment (they could be actually aliens, demons or angels) with the existentially crushing historical reality of slavery. It offers a redemptive counter-history for the standard accounts of the African diaspora.

Ra dwelt on the diaspora only obliquely and always subversively. For instance, he told an African well-wisher who welcomed him "home" upon his January 1977 arrival in Nigeria that "Your people sold mine. This is no longer my home!" (Szwed 342). He preferred to emphasize the pre-diasporic glories of ancient Egypt and Africa and the future promise of the space age. What happened between in the present and recent past was an unpleasant time of travail.

He explained his ambivalence about black folks, which he typically dissociated himself from, to poet Henry Dumas through the use of his linguistic "equations." "Negro" also referred to "Necro," the word for death, and "Ne-CROW," a black bird. From there Ra could leap to another black bird, Edgar Allen Poe's raven. "Quoth the Raven 'Nevermore.'" And "Raven" backwards is "naver," which sounds like "never" (*The Ark and the Ankh*). In Ra's cosmology, contemporary black people are semantically rhymed with death, birds of ill-omen and ill-repute, and the spirit of negation itself.

He had other critiques of this ethnicity as well. Ra called them "block people" because they hindered his career (Szwed 366). In the film *Space Is the Place*, he hires an African-American street wino at his "Outer Space Employment Agency" to do "nothing" and be paid "nothing" since his qualifications are "nothing." Ra explained in interview about the film's message that he wanted to work with "black folks because they're priceless. They have no price. They're worthless. They ain't worth nothing. Priceless. Give them to me. That's in the film" (Szwed 332). As noted above, Ra threatens in the film to drag them in chains into outer space, if necessary. Ra is not a gentle redeemer of this race which he dissociated himself from. He once told Alton Abraham: "I hate black people ... . I don't know about white people. I don't know any. But I know I hate black people" (Corbett 176).

In fuller context, however, these disparaging racist and even misanthropic remarks are only one side of a two-sided dialectical coin. Black people are worthless AND aliens, angels, demons in disguise; powerless and empowered; slaves AND pharaohs. Ra himself is from Saturn AND at times an African-American ("Your people sold *mine*," italics added). Every African-American intellectual has had to confront this double heritage / inheritance / identity of pride and shame: W.E.B. Du Bois, James Baldwin, Richard Wright, Paule Marshall, Toni Morrison, Malcolm X and, yes, James Brown. Ra's mythic rewrites of self, history, and ethnicity show how he negotiated these treacherous existential shoals, how he "got over." Who are we to gainsay his myths if we haven't had his experiences growing up in early twentieth-century Birmingham, Alabama?

Fortunately for Ra, he was not alone. He had a musical family and body of disciples: the Arkestra. Sun Ra has explicated some of the connotations of the name he gave his "outer space orchestra":

> "A covenant of Arkestra": it's like a selective service of God. Picking out some people. Arkestra has a "ra" at the beginning and the end ... . Ra can be written as "Ar" or "Ra," and on both ends of the word it is an equation: the first and the last are equal ... . That's phonetic balance ... . Besides, ... that's the way black people say "orchestra." (Szwed 94)

John Szwed adds a few other references besides the obvious one to the Ark of the Covenant. The Egyptian sun god Ra had a solar boat or ark. "Kest" in the middle of the name evokes "kist" as in "Sunkist"—kissed by the sun. In Sanskrit, "kist" means "sun's gleam" (94). I would additionally add the very obvious reference to Noah's ark: the Arkestra is on a mission to transport black people (and eventually all followers) safely to outer space before planetary destruction occurs. (This scenario is played out literally in the film *Space Is the Place*.) I also find Ra's reference to the selective service interesting, since he was a conscientious objector during World War II. Rather than play by the white man's rules, Ra devised an alternate draft for worthy musicians. This parallelism in effect resembles similar trends such as black freemasonry. I won't be the first to observe that the Arkestra in performance looked like extraterrestrial Shriners!

By now one can readily see that there was a great degree of esoteric doctrine and pedagogy behind the music and the visual cosmo-drama of this band in performance. Not surprisingly, Ra's mysterious presence spawned miraculous tales, some repeated enough with variations to suggest urban legends. There are many stories of the Arkestra's playing ostensibly causing electrical failures; Ra would even take such outages as indications that they "got it right" (Szwed 125). Most auspiciously, the lights in the Great Pyramid went out when Ra approached the King's Chamber on a tour (Szwed 293). Several accounts describe audience members claiming that the Arkestra was playing "God's music" or "the forbidden sacred music" of India. In these anecdotes, Ra always responds "That's what I hear" (Szwed 180, 221). Finally, Ed Michel (one of the band's producers) recounts the Ra contingent's ability to call him before he could dial a number to call them. He'd just pick up the phone, on numerous occasions, and they'd already be there (liner notes, *The Great Lost Sun Ra Albums*). All of this certainly adds to the legendary status of the band and its leader. Then there's the music itself, readily available from Amazon and other sellers, or on Youtube and Google.

Transition

You have just read the slightly revised opening sections of "We Travel Ra's Spaceways" from my 2013 book **Adventures in Avant-Pop**. I stand by everything I said here, but we will delve a lot deeper into Sun Ra's myth and mystery in the pages ahead. You also, dear reader, have a sense of my subject position as a devotee of Sun Ra — maybe beyond what you have even desired!

The next text I offer to you is my play **Discipline 27-II**, which was written in the spring and summer of 2013. As the postscript to the play will explain, this was an attempt to recast Sun Ra's life, art and ideas in dramatic form (as opposed to the approach of a cultural critic.) It had the extreme good fortune to be performed in St. Louis before this publication.

One additional teaser I will mention is that the Sun Ra / NASA interactions in the second act were consciously cobbled from the science fiction writer J.G. Ballard's interest in the space program and from recurrent buzz in the world of Ra, all unfortunately undocumented, that NASA was very interested in Sun Ra's advice. (We do know Ra contacted NASA, applying for money connected with art projects in space — a cultural wing of NASA. Or do we? His application form looks legitimate as reproduced in various sources, but its provenance is a bit peculiar since I have never heard of any other applications made to this odd and somewhat unlikely funding source.)

But imagine my surprise when I finally viewed the director's cut of Sun Ra's 1974 film **Space Is the Place**. The additional twenty minutes of blaxploitation soft core porn emphasized even more a subplot involving NASA employees shadowing Sun Ra and patronizing a brothel where they maul some of the sex workers. One can readily see why Ra vetoed this footage in the original release; but this version highlights much more the Ra / NASA connection that is overshadowed in the official film by the Ra / Overseer conflict. Such synchronicitous serendipities are almost inevitable when one tarries with the magnificent man from Saturn... .

Part II
Discipline-27-II

Discipline 27-II Set-Up

Dramatis Personae

Sun Ra, the living myth, on keyboards

Members of the Arkestra:

       June Tyson, vocals
       John Gilmore, tenor saxophone
       Marshall Allen, alto saxophone and flute
       Pat Patrick, baritone saxophone
       James Jacson, bassoon and percussion

Four aliens
Three Saturn Aliens, plus additional Saturn Aliens on Earth:
    Drexel
    Rorrg
Alabama judge
Wynonie Harris, a blues shouter

The band at the Peacock:

       Tommy "Buggs" Hunter, drums
       Red Holloway, tenor saxophone

Alton Abraham, fellow spiritual seeker and Afro-futurist
The Lintels (four doo wop singers)
Bartender at Slug's, a bar on New York's lower east side
Barfly at Slug's
NASA official
Gaia, the Earth Goddess

    Plus other members of the Arkestra, court officials, musicians with Wynonie Harris, strippers, musicians at the Peacock Club, bar patrons at Slug's, etc.

Parts can be doubled if necessary.

Scenes in the Play

Prologue

Act One (here interspersed with the Arkestra playing and other exposition)

Scene one: Birmingham, Alabama, late 1930s

Scene two: Alabama courtroom, early 1940s

Scene three: Nashville recording studio, spring of 1946

Scene four: the Peacock Club outside Chicago, 1947

Scene five: Sun Ra's apartment on the South Side of Chicago, 1955

Scene six: same as previous scene, 1960

Act Two

Scene one: Slug's, a bar on New York's lower east side, 1969

Scene two: the House of Ra, Philadelphia, a month later

Scene three: a stage in Orlando, Florida, slightly later

Discipline 27-II: A Cosmo-Drama in Two Acts

Induction / introduction to the play:

This work will simultaneously tell the story of Sun Ra and offer a facsimile of a Sun Ra concert. To replicate the latter, total theatre is optimal (if the production can afford it). The audience should be in a Sun Ra space (pun intended) the moment their tickets are torn and they enter the theater, Here are some suggestions for achieving those results.

In the lobby:

Members of the cast who will not be needed to play on stage before the play starts (see below) should be at some utility tables. They should be in costumes reminiscent of Sun Ra's Arkestra. The easiest way for a costume designer to accomplish this is to study the abundant visual evidence of the band's "look" on album covers, videos and the internet. Shriner effects, the costumes of Black Masonry, colorful felt hats and an abundance of colored metal foil are a rough approach to this part of the *mise-en-scene*.

They can be selling Sun Ra CDs either at cost or to make a modest profit to donate to the actual living members of the Arkestra, most quite elderly, who live at 5626 Morton Street / Philadelphia, PA 19144. Other merchandise if available is great: Sun Ra's books, vinyl, t-shirts, jewelry.

Sun Ra's "Moon Stew" (which he fed the band on in tough times) may also be sold as a concession or given away to the patrons. Here is the recipe obtained from the internet. Bear in mind that there are no specific measurements involved. As Sun Ra notes,

> You can't say "One teaspoon of this, or one teaspoon of that." Like a musician, you have to improvise. It's like being on a spirit plane; you put the proper things in without knowing why. It comes out wonderful when it's done like that. If you plan it, it doesn't work.

Here are the ingredients:

- Green peppers
- Onions
- Garlic
- Potatoes
- Okra
- Tomatoes
- Corn
- Flour
- Butter or Vegetable Oil
- Broth (chicken or vegetable)
- Salt and Pepper to taste
- Sincerity
- Love

To prepare:

Chop the vegetables.

Bring the broth to a simmer on the stove while making a roux. To make the roux, melt the butter or vegetable oil in a pan and add flour, stirring until it reaches the consistency of wet sand. Stir a little of the broth into the roux and then add the roux to the broth.

Add the vegetables, salt, pepper, sincerity and love to the broth.

Cook for at least one hour, stirring occasionally, tasting and adding ingredients as needed for culinary improvisation.

Induction / introduction to the play:

On the stage:

As the audience members arrive, the stage lights should already be on and the house lights down. Actor / musicians in suitable costumes are on the stage already, improvising gently on stringed instruments. The more exotic, the better: African koras, kotos, lutes, zithers, harps, string dulcimers. There should be already in place musical setups for keyboards, drums, etc.

Since the number of members in the Arkestra varied, the director will have to work with the resources at hand. But everyone in the Arkestra will need (at least ideally) to have some competence, however modest, as both an actor and a jazz musician. The easiest way to solve the problem of playing the more difficult actual Sun Ra compositions would be to have either a pit orchestra or use recordings of the real band. Then the onstage musicians can fake their playing. Ideally, one could have for some productions people on stage who could actually play everything. The Arkestra should have at least seven members and could go as high as fifteen—or even above!

The theater should open at least twenty minutes before the actual beginning of the show. As the starting time approaches, other musicians should file in: reeds, horns, percussionists (as available). This music, like the Moon Stew, is totally improvised. There should be no recognizable melodies. The only ground rules are that the musicians should listen to and dialogue with each other, play off the feel of the audience (what mood are they in? did some good or bad event happen on the world stage and/or locally?) and gradually build in intensity (tempo, loudness) so that by the starting time of the play the music is almost painfully loud, raucous, dissonant.

At an off-stage hand signal or dramatic on-stage noise like the banging of a gong, all the instruments should cease playing except for one or two percussionists who switch to a simple beat appropriate for the first chant, "Waiting for the Sunrise."

Prologue

The actress playing JUNE TYSON comes out and steps up to the microphone.

JUNE TYSON : The world is waiting for the sunrise, for the sunrise, for the sunrise.

> *She sings this several times; on the third pass, the other members of the THE ARKESTRA join in for a few more iterations. Some nights the audience might also join in; one could even put in "plants" for that purpose to encourage participation. When JUNE TYSON raises her hands (at somewhere between four and seven repetitions), ALL the music stops.*

JUNE TYSON (*sings a cappella*):

> When the world was in darkness
> And darkness was ignorance
> Along came Ra

OTHER MEMBERS OF THE ARKESTRA : Along came Ra

JUNE TYSON :

> When the world was in darkness
> And darkness was ignorance
> Along came Ra

THE ARKESTRA : Along came Ra

JUNE TYSON :

> The living myth
> The living myth
> The living mystery
> The living myth
> The living myth
> The living mystery

THE ARKESTRA onstage, pit band or tape begins playing "Discipline 27-II." SUN RA walks out from stage left. He should be dressed resplendently along the lines of available imagery. The actor who plays him should be of portly girth (or willing to wear a "fat suit"). All of his moves onstage should be regal, even portentous. SUN RA is after all the living myth, a pharaoh, a representative of the sun and the greater omniverse. He walks to center stage and spreads his arms.

SUN RA :

Some call me Mister Ra
Some call me Mister E
But you can call me Mister Mystery

He turns his back to the audience and exhorts the band to play even more intensely. The band in whatever arrangement plays the theme for several minutes while SUN RA prowls the stage.

SUN RA : This world is not my home, is not my home, is not my home. This world is not my home, is not my home, is not my home. Why would I come from a planet of death? I said, why would I come from a planet of death? If you were born here, you have to die here! I come from the greater universe. The universe has sent me to converse with you.

The band plays on as the stage lights fade. A screen is needed for the next part. It could be lowered or just set up at the back of the stage. Or one could use a scrim. SUN RA could be narrating this portion live or on tape, since the actor who plays SUN RA will be changing into street clothes, ca. late 1930s to early 1940s. THE ARKESTRA music should also fade, perhaps to be replaced by a tape of big band jazz—ideally Fletcher Henderson.

While SUN RA narrates, historic slides of Birmingham, Alabama should be projected on the screen. The director has a lot of leeway here, but some bases should definitely be touched: Terminal Station and the old "Magic City" sign, Tuxedo Junction, motorcycle cops in a row in front of Legion Field, any photos of African Americans and the black business district, the pig iron blast furnaces that were the city's original source of growth and wealth, the statue of Vulcan and the Temple of Sibyl. (These last two to show that the city had a certain tolerance for myth!) Todd Keith's **Birmingham Then and Now** *(San Diego: Thunder Bay Press, 2008) will have most of what the production will need. Or just surf the internet.*

Prologue

SUN RA : I arrived here on May 22, 1914. I wasn't born, because whoever is born has to die. Birth with an "i" points to berth with an "e," which is be-earthed, doomed to be on Earth, which is not for me. Or for you. I arrived in Birmingham, Alabama, which is the Magic City so I grew up surrounded by magic and learned how to practice it, you see. There was a statue of Vulcan the forger god at the state fairgrounds to remind everyone of the magic that made the city rise up from two train crossings in a field to make pig iron from the minerals in the surrounding hills. Some white man built a temple to other Greek gods up on another hill.

And I grew up right near Terminal Station, the largest train station in the South. That's magic too, all them trains coming through: the Black Diamond Express, the Sunset Limited, the City of New Orleans. Magic to ride on them, magic to see them whoosh by, magic to flatten them pennies that you put on the tracks if you had any to spare.

There was lots of music in my life always, bands you heard of and natural beauty you couldn't believe if I told you, joyful noise that blossomed like a flower and then faded away to just a memory. For a long, long time I never saw any white people close up. Back then blacks and whites didn't mix at all. They had that temple on the hill and their good seats in the movie shows; we had music, you see. That's why music was so important to black people. It was almost all we had, and it was free. Sound is free. I can make you pay to hear my sounds, but I don't have to pay nothing to make them after I get the instrument. Back then you didn't even have to pay for the electricity because musical instruments didn't need it.

So I never saw white people really, but I did see black people.

Act One

Scene 1

>*The actor playing SUN RA steps out on stage in street clothes. A single spotlight shines on him. The slide projector is turned off.*

SUN RA : And then, one day, I saw my people—and they saw me. Except, you see, like me, they weren't people at all.

>*Big band jazz (if playing) fades. Spooky space sounds are heard from a synthesizer on stage or a recording (the music from the original **The Day the Earth Stood Still** or **Forbidden Planet** would do nicely).*

>*Aliens enter from the back of the theater. The director has a lot of leeway here as well. These can be new actors or doubled parts from THE ARKESTRA members. They can be dressed just like THE ARKESTRA was or have additional alien features (like the classic grey alien mask). Or experiment with another look—as long as they connote the alien and don't look like ordinary people. They should each be carrying a miniature laser (like the ones you buy as a pet toy or at a novelty shop). Before actually walking down the aisles, they should announce their entrance by flashing the lasers above the heads of the audience onto the stage. (Avoid hitting anyone in the eye.) As they approach the stage, they should concentrate their laser beams on SUN RA (below the neck).*

>*They walk in a slow and stately manner, then mount the stage and surround SUN RA.*

FIRST ALIEN : Are you the one we seek?

SECOND ALIEN : Do you want to travel to outer space?

THIRD ALIEN : Do you have perfect discipline?

SUN RA : I need to see what you want to show me. I've never fit in on this planet.

A second spotlight comes on downstage.

FOUR ALIENS : Step into that beam.

FIRST ALIEN : There is some danger involved.

THIRD ALIEN : You must keep your body inside the beam as long as it is on.

SECOND ALIEN : If you step out of the beam you will be scattered through several time zones.

FOURTH ALIEN : You will be transmolecularized. You will be able to see through your body.

FIRST ALIEN : But do not be alarmed.

FOURTH ALIEN : You may now step into the beam.

SUN RA steps into the beam. The stage goes completely dark, but the space sounds continue. On the screen we see slides of the planet Saturn gradually increasing in size. In the last few images a railroad track narrowing into the horizon is superimposed on the planet.

Then the projector is turned off and the light comes up on a boxing ring with different aliens in it and a painted simulation on stage of rows of seats going up like a sports stadium. These aliens can look any way desired except for one detail: they have metal antennae projecting from their ears and above their eyes. (Any metal rod will serve for this effect: barbecue skewers, unlit sparklers, etc,) The painted backdrop need not be especially elaborate or even realistic. Go for broad, simple strokes in set design. Meanwhile the actor playing SUN RA has taken a seat in the back of the actual theater.

CHORUS OF SATURN ALIENS : Where are you, traveler? Come down here and join us. Herman? Herman Blount? Snookum?

They flash their lasers on SUN RA.

CHORUS OF ALIENS : We see you. Come down here.

SUN RA walks down the aisle and onto the stage and into the ring.

FIRST SATURN ALIEN : So what are you doing on planet Earth?

SUN RA : I'm going to a teacher's college in Alabama. I want to be a teacher of men.

Act I.i

SECOND SATURN ALIEN : When you return to Earth, stop that training.

THIRD SATURN ALIEN : There's going to be great trouble in schools. There's going to be trouble in every part of life. Don't have anything to do with it. Don't continue.

SECOND SATURN ALIEN : When it seems like the world is going into complete chaos, when there's no hope for nothing, then you may speak—and the world will listen. Until then, say nothing.

> *Blackout. Slides of Saturn receding and Earth approaching. When the lights come up, both the SATURN ALIENS and the other ALIENS are present surrounding SUN RA. They put a robe on him (most conveniently, the one he wore when he first came out).*

FIRST SATURN ALIEN (*gestures out to the actual audience*): Go out there and speak to them. Now is your time.

SUN RA : No, they look like they're angry. I'm not going out there.

FIRST ALIEN : They aren't angry, they're bewildered.

> *Toy flying saucers drop from the ceiling on wires. (They can even be painted paper plates a la Ed Wood.) The ceiling is lit purple and dark red above them.*

ALIENS IN UNISON : You can order us to land. Are conditions right for landing?

(*Pause.*)

SUN RA : Yes.

> *All lights drop except for the single spotlight on SUN RA. Stagehands remove what needs to be taken away.*

SUN RA : They started to land, and there were people running to come to the landing, and they shot something like bullets. But they weren't bullets. They were something that when they hit the ground they were like chewing gum. They stuck people to the ground.

(*Pause.*)

SUN RA : I came out of that vision. Those things have been indelibly printed on my brain. I couldn't get them out if I tried.

> *Lights come up on stage to reveal THE ARKESTRA performing "Discipline 27-II" again. They vamp for a few minutes.*

SUN RA (*over music*): I am the sun. I greet you every morning. Good morning, my friends. Every day the wind my brother and I invite you to outer space. We wait to hear you say "Please let me try something else than Planet Earth." 'Cause down here you try and die. You try and die. Why don't you be like us?

(*Pause.*)

SUN RA : I use planets for stepping stones.

THE ARKESTRA : Stepping stones, stepping stones, stepping stones.

SUN RA : I said, I use planets for stepping stones.

THE ARKESTRA : Stepping stones, stepping stones, stepping stones.

SUN RA : If you can't be men on this planet, be angels. They are not condemned to die like men.

Lights fade; music fades more slowly for a scene change to a courtroom in Alabama. Lights come up.

Scene 2

ALABAMA JUDGE : Will Herman Poole Blount step up to the bench?

SUN RA approaches the bench in street clothes.

ALABAMA JUDGE : Are you Herman Poole Blount?

SUN RA : Some people call me that.

ALABAMA JUDGE : What do you call yourself?

SUN RA : It depends on what and how I'm feeling. Sometimes I'm "Sonny," but sometimes I might just also be "Satan."

ALABAMA JUDGE : Nigger, are you trying to mess around with me?

SUN RA : No, your honor, I'm just trying to give you an honest answer to your question.

ALABAMA JUDGE : This court will not tolerate any sass from an uppity nee-gro. Be advised accordingly.

Now let's review your case here. It says that you have been granted a provisional 4-E status as a conscientious objector opposed to both combatant and noncombatant military service. On what grounds do you oppose the war?

SUN RA : As a Christian, I oppose fighting and killing of any kind. "Thou shalt not kill" is one of the ten commandments God handed down to Moses. Do you want me to give you chapters and verses here?

Act I.ii 49

ALABAMA JUDGE : That won't be necessary. I am quite familiar with the Bible as a Southern Baptist.

SUN RA : Then you know that the Old and the New Testaments agree on this. Just like the Old forbids killing, Jesus says in the New one to love your enemies and turn the other cheek to them if they strike you.

ALABAMA JUDGE : And yet many Christians are fighting in this war.

SUN RA : That's right but they're sinning, you see. The Jews in the Old Testament killed some of their enemies, and that was a sin too. The Bible is extremely clear as to what you should do.

ALABAMA JUDGE : What church do you belong to?

SUN RA : I don't belong to any church because the men who run them lack discipline. But I am a Christian and I study and follow my Bible. I've thought about being a Seventh Day Adventist. I admire that church the most.

ALABAMA JUDGE : I can order you to serve your country or go to prison.

SUN RA : You can do that, but I don't think that would be a good thing. See, I don't know how to kill yet. If they train me to kill, I'll do a good job because I have precision and discipline. I'm good at whatever I try to do, like playing and writing music. I won't be prejudiced about who I kill either. I'll kill the first person who I run into, who just might be a captain or a general in my own army.

In any case, I got nothing against the Germans or the Italians or the Japanese. I don't have the right to go and fight with those people. They never even struck me; I never had to turn my cheek.

Living here in Alabama, your honor, you know who Negroes have to turn the other cheek to, who strikes them again and again. It's not the Germans or the Italians or the Japanese. Now I turn the other cheek. But if they train me to kill, I'll kill anyone whose path I cross, especially if they oppress me in any way. So, you see, it's better to let sleeping dogs lie sometimes.

ALABAMA JUDGE : I've never seen a nigger like you before.

SUN RA : No. And you never will again.

ALABAMA JUDGE : This court sentences you to be held in Walker County Jail until we can make a final ruling on your draft status. Case dismissed.

>*Lights fade. Music comes up. We are back with THE ARKESTRA playing "Discipline 27-II" for a few bars.*

SUN RA : You're on the right road, but you're going in the wrong direction.

I say, you're on the right road, but you're going in the wrong direction. Earth is a cursed and doomed planet. The truth about the nations of planet Earth is a bad truth.

THE ARKESTRA : A BAAD TRUTH!

SUN RA : The truth about the history of the people of planet Earth is a bad truth.

THE ARKESTRA : IT'S A BAAD TRUTH!

> *SUN RA begins to march around the stage followed by members of the band who set down their instruments and march in a circle with him. Drums keep a martial beat, but the rest of the music ceases.*

SUN RA : Shoulder to shoulder

> Man to man
> March as men should
> March as men should
>
> *(repeat chant five times; THE ARKESTRA members do a call and response repetition of each phrase)*

SUN RA (*stops marching; band goes back to instruments but only vamps a little*): Fight against the common enemy of all mankind, namely DEAAATTTH!

> Don't be a slave.
> Lay down in the grave.
> Bow down in the dust.

(*repeat three times*)

When you travel through outer space, you must use the password, the word of victory: Ra!

THE ARKESTRA : Ra! Ra! Ra! Ra! Ra! Ra!

SUN RA : You're just babies in the universe. I could've enjoyed myself on this planet if the people had been alive.

Scene 3

> *Stage goes black. WYNONIE HARRIS ' "Dig This Boogie" plays while SUN RA changes into street clothes (and other actors, if parts are being doubled). Lights come up on a recording studio in Nashville, spring of 1946. The only instruments that need to be around are drums, upright bass, trumpet and piano for SUN RA. There is a standing microphone for the vocalist as well. Musicians, SUN RA*

Act I.iii

> (now in ordinary clothes) and WYNONIE HARRIS enter. WYNONIE HARRIS is a dapper, well-dressed tall light-skinned African American. The actor playing him should definitely be of a lighter skin tone than SUN RA, although cosmetics may be used to achieve this effect. WYNONIE HARRIS ' hair should be slicked back with hair oil.

WYNONIE HARRIS : I dug that boogie, Sonny. You sure can play that real barrelhouse boogie. Where'd you learn to play like that?

SUN RA : I been playing all my life, as far back as I can remember I guess. I'm trying to get a club gig in Chicago.

WYNONIE HARRIS : Well, I'm sure glad you joined that Chicago musician's union so I could bring you down here.

> (Pause.)

WYNONIE HARRIS : What do you say. boys? Shall we lay down one more for Bullet records to make Jim Bulleit rich from all the money colored folks are gonna be sliding into those Seeburg jukeboxes? I wrote a real hot blues number called "Lightnin' Struck the Poor House." I'll give you some chords here (*hands them out*). It's pretty standard blues changes.

As always, I work in a little fun stuff in the lyrics. The song could be about a guy forced out onto the street because the poor house he was in got struck by lightning in a storm. Or....

> *WYNONIE HARRIS pulls out a flask and takes a drink.*

WYNONIE HARRIS : ... he could be lamenting that somebody's running white lightnin' like this and he don't have a dime to buy it—which is maybe why his old lady is treating him so mean. She wants him to buy her a taste. Or maybe he's broke because he spent all his money on the moonshine.

> *WYNONIE HARRIS drinks again.*

WYNONIE HARRIS : I need this stuff for my throat, but it might help y'all's playing as well. Sonny, you want a blast?

> *He offers the flask to SUN RA.*

SUN RA : No thanks, Mr. Harris. I don't drink.

WYNONIE HARRIS : A hot piano player like you that wants to play in Chicago clubs don't drink? Why on earth not?

SUN RA : It was drink that ruined things for black people, you see.

WYNONIE HARRIS : You mean it keeps us down and out?

SUN RA : Oh, it's much worse than that, Mr. Harris. Noah's son Ham in the Bible saw his daddy naked because Noah had been drinking, you see. So Noah cursed Ham and his children and Ham was the founder of the black race. So if there wouldn't have been no drinking the black race would never have been cursed like they were. And part of that curse is all them colored folks drinking, which leads to them cutting and shooting and razor fighting and fornicating.

Just for me, personally, you see, alcoholic drinks are how you let the devil in your door. And once he gets in, you don't know what he's going to encourage you to do to please him. So that's why I don't even let him in that way. I deny him the entrance. I do like to let the devil in sometimes so we can chat about things, but I don't want to give him that advantage right off. We're on an even footing if I don't drink much besides water.

WYNONIE HARRIS : Damn, Sonny, you got quite a point of view. I never heard a temperance rap put that way.

SUN RA : It's just what I've come to figure out. You can take it or leave it.

WYNONIE HARRIS : I believe I'll take another pull for my golden voice. Anybody else?

One or two other musicians take a drink.

WYNONIE HARRIS : All right, mister engineer. Let's roll that tape. One, two, one two three, go.

The band starts playing. They can either do the song or fake it with a tape. SUN RA, of course, is on piano.

WYNONIE HARRIS :

>Lightnin' struck the poor house
>Poor me I didn't have a dime
>Yes, lightnin' struck the poor house
>Poor me I didn't have a dime
>Ain't got no money
>And my baby won't give me none of her time
>
>I may be down
>I'll raise up before long
>Yes I may be down baby
>But I'll raise up before long
>And you'll be looking for me

Act I.iii

And I'll be long, long gone

Well, you can sing out your hymn book
Preach out your Bible
Get on your knees and pray to the good Lord above

But I say baby
You gonna need my help someday
Well, you gonna call on me
But I'll be so far, far away

Lights fade. Costume changes are made back into THE ARKESTRA garb. "Discipline 27-II" fades in as the lights go up. Repeat the instrumental vamp for a while.

SUN RA :

I am the king of the kingdom of mystery.
I am the king of the kingdom of mystery.
I have many names.
Names of splendor.
Names of shame.
One of my names ... is Sin.

SUN RA (cont'd):

When the lights are low, what do they do?
They SIIIIIIIN!
When they close the door, and the lights are low, what do they do?
They SIIIIIIIN!

I am Sin.
Everybody loves me.
I bring them pleasure without measure.

I can't stand it.
All those people in love with me.
SIIIIIIIN!
Five million people in love with me.
Because I'm SIIIIIIIIN!

Lights and music fade. Fade in any jazz standard for trio (piano, drums and tenor saxophone). SUN RA changes into street clothes. Move in two dividers that split the stage area into thirds.

Perhaps angle the dividers so the audience can see their purposes. We are in a strip club, the Peacock in Calumet City, Illinois, in 1947. One divider is the "Iron Curtain" to keep black men from seeing white flesh.

Scene 4: Peacock Club, Chicago 1947

On stage right, in fact, a strip tease is going on to the music. The director can carry this as far as possible, although credibility demands that the striptease go no further than pasties and a G-string. The DANCER must be white, but no particular age (as long as it's a legal age!) or body type is necessary. She should not directly face the actual audience since we are getting a side view of the proceedings.

In the center third, the trio is playing (live or to a tape): SUN RA on piano, TOMMY "BUGGS" HUNTER on drums and RED HOLLOWAY on tenor sax.

Stage left is simply a cluttered backstage area for the musicians to hang out.

When the DANCER finishes and leaves, the three musicians walk over to the backstage area as three more musicians come in—and another stripper. (The show never stops.) The music and dancing continue, but the former gradually fades so we can hear the spoken dialogue. Eventually the second DANCER will be practically miming her dance. The director should feel free to add surrealistic or expressionistic touches here. The goal is a sordid form of total theatre while the plot is advanced on stage left.

The band members towel off. TOMMY "BUGGS" HUNTER and RED HOLLOWAY reach for beers; SUN RA pours a glass of ice water from a pitcher. They sip throughout.

RED HOLLOWAY : Man, what a grindhouse.

TOMMY "BUGGS" HUNTER : And they won't even let us see the ladies.

RED HOLLOWAY : As if we even want to go near that mess. When those ofay girls sweat, they smell like wet dogs in the rain.

TOMMY "BUGGS" HUNTER : Or like chickens.

All laugh.

Act I.iv

SUN RA : Nonetheless, we're doing the right thing playing this gig.

TOMMY "BUGGS" HUNTER : How so, Sonny?

SUN RA : Well, there are two major powers warring in the universe: God and the devil. If you don't want bad things to happen to you, you should always be trying to please one or the other of them. If you don't do that, no cosmic forces will be on your side looking out for you. I found that there are very few things that you can do which please both God and the devil. Playing music at the Peacock Club is one of them.

RED HOLLOWAY : How are we doing that?

SUN RA : Well, the Creator likes discipline, especially for musicians because we pass on the harmonies of the universe. Look at all the hundreds of songs we've learned to play here: "Begin the Beguine," "King Porter Stomp," "Stardust," "Limehouse Blues," "Big John's Special," "Tea for Two," "Caravan," "Stranger in Paradise." That pleases the Creator.

And the devil likes that we're helping white men sin. They shoot their seed at those women—and into them if they're lucky or rich. And they don't necessarily stop at the deadly sin of lust. If those girls have boyfriends, the devil might get to see some fighting or killing too. He likes all of that. And they're drinking and getting drunk here too. It's easy to commit every sin you can imagine when you're drunk. And drunkenness itself is a form of gluttony, another deadly sin.

Plus we get paid very well to play here. And money is a useful tool for the devil. Almost half the ways to spend money on this planet are evil—whether you're buying some whiskey or even eating a candy bar that isn't good for your body, a temple the Lord made.

That's why the Bible says that money is the root of all evil. You can do good things with money, like give it away to the poor so they can eat. Not everything money does is evil; but every evil comes from that root of money somehow. Back to those white men here: they had to pay a cover charge to see those titties. It wasn't free. You see?

TOMMY "BUGGS" HUNTER : So if we're pleasing God and the devil, are they going to reward us?

SUN RA : Things will happen to us that you can't even imagine. We won't be playing here for long. The whole world will know what we do. You just have to discover and explore your alter-destiny. You have to wait to find fate in a pleasant mood.

Lights fade. "Discipline 27-II" comes back up. SUN RA changes into full costume while THE ARKESTRA vamps. He returns to the front of the stage and speaks while the music plays.

SUN RA : If I told you that I was from outer space, you wouldn't believe a word I said.

> Would you?
> Why should you?
> You lost your way.
> You should have nothing to say.
> You can't go to Saturn.
> You can't go anyplace.
> You're living in shame.
> You're bound to die.

> *SUN RA descends from the stage and walks up to a random member of the audience and puts his hands on their shoulders.*

SUN RA : GIVE UP YOUR DEATH TO ME!

> *He remounts the stage.*

SUNRA AND THE ARKESTRA together:

> We come from nowhere here.
> Why can't we go somewhere there?
> We come from nowhere here.
> Why can't we go somewhere there?
> We come from nowhere here.
> Why can't we go somewhere there?

> *Lights and music fade while SUN RA gets back into street clothes. The lights gradually come up on an apartment, Chicago's south side, 1955. There is a piano in the room and a lot of books and papers (which can be placed there and/or suggested through painted backdrops). A few chairs which the actors can sit on—or not—and a table. The director has some freedom here as to how to best block the scene as the conversation flows. SUN RA can be sitting on a chair or at the piano when a knock is heard. On the side of the stage there is some suggestion of a door.*

Scene 5: Sun Ra's Apartment, Chicago 1955

> *SUN RA gets up and answers it. In walks ALTON ABRAHAM, a very handsome and lean African American in formal attire (dress pants, white shirt, tie and suit) with a Russian style hat on his head.*

Act I.v 57

> *He is carrying books and broadsheets. He runs El Saturn Research and Infinity, Inc., businesses designed to propagate respectively SUN RA's music and ideas.*

ALTON ABRAHAM : Are you busy, Sonny?

SUN RA : I have a street corner doo wop group coming over to rehearse, but they're on colored people's time. They don't have much discipline. So set yourself down. Who knows when they'll be here?

> *ALTON ABRAHAM puts his materials on a table and sits down.*

ALTON ABRAHAM : Have I ever heard them?

SUN RA : I don't know. I caught them singing on one of the corners of the park by the speaker's corner. They're real young and wild. I gave them a name, the Lintels, to encourage them to think they could be on the threshold of something. Maybe you could put out a 45 of them on Saturn if I get them sounding good enough.

ALTON ABRAHAM : We could do that. Doo wop sells better than our space music. We could rob Peter to pay Paul.

> *(Pause.)*

ALTON ABRAHAM : I brought some things over for you. I copied some of your Bible leaflets for you to give out. And I found a few new books on ancient Egypt you might be interested in. Oh, and there's a book by a guy in California named George Adamski who says he's been taken aboard a flying saucer.

SUN RA : That sounds real interesting. The aliens that visited me in Alabama didn't use a saucer because it would have taken too long to get to Saturn that way, I guess. But they use flying saucers a lot. And have for a long time. You got Ezekiel's wheel in the Bible and some strong indications that they met the Egyptians and showed them how to build the pyramids and the Great Sphinx.

ALTON ABRAHAM : These could all be crucial connections for our black space program.

SUN RA : Yeah, we got to get the black folks back into space, and we sure can't rely on the white man to do it. You see the pictures of those air force test pilots they're training to be astronauts, and there's not a dark face among them.

ALTON ABRAHAM : The white race learned their lesson from those Tuskegee Airmen.

SUN RA : The Red Tails!

Both laugh.

SUN RA : They salted those tails. That's probably why they started doing them experiments at Tuskegee with syphilis. Last thing they want is uppity black men.

ALTON ABRAHAM : Especially in Alabama, as you well know!

SUN RA : So it's up to us. It's going to happen in phases. These pamphlets will help black folks understand the codes of the Bible and see how the Christian religion is designed to keep them in their place by following the cross's way of death. Then we'll gradually get them ready to go to other worlds with the music, which will also summon the aliens. Let me show you something.

He walks to the piano, sits down and plays a harmonious chord.

SUN RA : See, that's Earth music. But that won't please listeners from other planets who might be sitting in the audience.

He bangs a dissonant cluster of notes.

SUN RA : Now that might please somebody from Mars.

He plays another dissonant cluster.

SUN RA : And that might be good music on Jupiter. I've been transcribing these combinations, you see. I think we can find some musicians in this town who can play the space music. Don't worry; we'll have something for the Earth people too. But we have to run up a flag so the visitors know we know they're out there. And we're ready for them to land, just like I saw in my vision.

ALTON ABRAHAM : And we can get the records distributed, so the music can be heard outside of Chicago.

SUN RA : Eventually we should tour too.

ALTON ABRAHAM : A cosmic Chitlin' Circuit!

Both laugh.

SUN RA : I think the whole world will want to hear this music. We'll disguise it as jazz because Charlie Parker and everybody's getting them confused as to what jazz ought to be in the first place. Ears are opening. We need to give them a big show too. I learned at the Peacock Club that what you see matters as much as what you hear.

ALTON ABRAHAM : We'll build a musical Trojan horse to bring out the aliens waiting for a sign. The world governments will never know what hit them.

Act I.v

SUN RA : Right now they're trying to cover all this up.

ALTON ABRAHAM : But like Shakespeare says, "murder will out." We'll get out the truth through the back door.

> *Another knock on door.*

SUN RA : That must be the Lintels. You should probably go, because they're real shy kids for all of their toughness. They won't want to sing in front of you till they have it down perfect.

ALTON ABRAHAM : All right. See you, Sonny.

> *He leaves as the THE LINTELS come in. They exchange nods. SUN RA leads them over to the piano. The THE LINTELS are four scruffy black teenagers.*

SUN RA : Alright, boys. Last week we worked through "C'est Si Bon," "Blue Moon," "Baby Please Be Mine" and "Blue Skies." You feel good about those numbers?

FIRST LINTEL : Yeah, we been doing them on the corner and filling the hat.

SUN RA : So what do you want to do today?

SECOND LINTEL : We got a new song.

THIRD LINTEL : We want you to hear it and tell us if you like it and if there's ways we can make it better.

SUN RA : Well sing it to me. Do you need me to play anything on piano?

SECOND LINTEL : We're not sure. Let's just sing it to you first. It's called "My Only Love."

> *[The song can be heard on **Spaceship Lullaby** in the **Unheard Music Series** on Atavistic CD.]*

THE LINTELS : Nome-i-nome-i-nome-nome-dah-diddy-diddy *(3 times, then repeated continually as background chant)*

> Wop-whoaoaoah
>
> You are
> My only love
> Like the stars up above
> You my only love
>
> Each night I dream
> Of holding you tight
> Of kissing you goodnight

THE LINTELS (cont'd):

> You my only love
>
> Whoaoaoah *(4 times)*
>
> I-I-I-I-I
> I love you so
> Never let you go
> You my only love
>
> Whoaoaoah *(4 times)*
>
> Pause.

FIRST LINTEL : So what do you think?

SUN RA : I hear a lot of sincerity and divine simplicity in that. I'm not sure if piano—or anything, really—would add to the purity of the experience. But I'll think about possible arrangements.

> You might make it big some day. But keep on working in school, just in case.

VARIOUS LINTELS : Yes sir. We sure will, etc.

SUN RA : And, I know it's hard on that street corner, but stay away from that drugs and liquor. It will get you into all kinds of trouble. I've seen what it does to musicians all too often.

VARIOUS LINTELS : Yes sir. We know they bad, etc.

SUN RA : Don't you even smoke no tobacco. It'll ruin your fine voices.

> *(Pause.)*

SUN RA : The key to life, and music, you see, is discipline. You got to practice every day, like I do, and study— not just music, but the Bible and history and science. Then you'll be able to cut everybody else on that corner—and even conquer the world. For real. Now you boys get to your homework while I think about what we can do with your song.

SECOND LINTEL : Thanks for your time and advice, mister. We sure do appreciate it.

> *They leave. Lights dim to black. One of the SATURN ALIENS comes out on stage right. "Interplanetary Music" plays on tape, followed by "Lights on a Satellite" and "El is the Sound of Joy," etc., as needed throughout the slideshow. A screen is made available to project slides.*

Act I.v 61

SATURN ALIENS : All we had hoped for came to pass. Herman "Sonny" Blount had his name officially changed to Sun Ra. And he had his space orchestra, the Arkestra. Because the economy improved, he could afford a bigger band than the small combos necessitated by the gas shortages of your second great war and its recovery.

> *Pause.*

ALIEN : Yes, we keep a close watch on your race. We always have and we always will.

> *Pause.*

ALIEN : There was Robert Barry, the drummer.

> *Slide of him.*

ALIEN : Pat Patrick on baritone saxophone, a loyal and sensitive player who would stay with Sun Ra through thick and thin.

> *Slide of PAT PATRICK.*

ALIEN : Most amazingly, John Gilmore, one of the most innovative and versatile tenor saxes in the history of jazz. Because of his willingness to be Sun Ra's musical disciple, he was never accorded the respect and recognition on Earth that he deserved. John Gilmore was a major influence on the much better known John Coltrane. Gilmore showed John Coltrane some of the secret space chords Sun Ra used to communicate with us. Like many great musicians, John Gilmore learned from the birds and their songs.

> *Slide of JOHN GILMORE.*

ALIEN : There was Richard Evans on bass.

> *Slide of THE ARKESTRA at the Parkway Ballroom in Chicago in 1955. ALIEN uses laser pointer to indicate RICHARD EVANS.*

ALIEN : Julian Priester on trombone.

> *Laser points to him.*

ALIEN : In time, James Jacson on bassoon.

> *Slide of him.*

ALIEN : Crucially, Marshall Allen on alto saxophone and flute, destined to lead the band for many years after Sun Ra left Earth.

> *Slide of him.*

ALIEN : And many more great tone scientists. They played all over Chicago in the mid to late 1950s.

While he talks, slides of the fifties ARKESTRA are shown.

ALIEN : The Parkway Ballroom, the Wonder Inn, Budland, the Grand Ballroom. Jazz musicians and intellectuals came to hear their sound.

Slide of author Norman Mailer.

ALIEN : Anybody out there in the audience know who this dude is?

If anyone guesses correctly, the alien should give them some kind of space age or SUN RA themed door prize!

[*If they guess the name, add the following line of dialogue:*

ALIEN : That's right, Norman Mailer.]

[*if not, say this:*

ALIEN : It's Norman Mailer.]

In either case:

ALIEN : Norman Mailer isn't too well-known now, but he was a famous American writer after World War II. He wrote a great novel *The Naked and the Dead* about his fighting the Japanese. And he wrote an essay in the 1950s called "The White Negro" which said that African American culture was the only real American culture worth paying any attention to; the rest was just watered-down Europe. So Norman Mailer had to go check out Sun Ra and his Arkestra and the space music when he visited Chicago.

But here's the kicker: he was sick with a cold and congestion. After hearing the band, he said the space music completely cured his cold. Isn't that interesting? I think it is even if you earthlings might not.

(Laughs.)

ALIEN : But Sun Ra knew a wider audience was waiting out there—the rest of planet Earth and many other worlds both known and unknown. Strange worlds.

Lights come up on SUN RA's apartment, the same as in previous scene. We see ALTON ABRAHAM, SUN RA, JOHN GILMORE and MARSHALL ALLEN in street clothes in various positions talking.

Scene 6: same, 1960

ALTON ABRAHAM : Sonny, I think you should definitely take the job at the Mocambo in Montreal. Chicago is no longer much interested in you. You were in their eyes a novelty act good for a little press. But they don't see you're serious, that you're a serious musician and philosopher.

SUN RA : I guess you're right. We're never going to get new listeners if we just stay here. We have to promote those recordings.

ALTON ABRAHAM : And that producer Tom Wilson said he'd hook you up with club dates and a place to stay if you came to New York.

MARSHALL ALLEN : We could just swing through Canada and cross back over at Niagara Falls, then head down to New York.

JOHN GILMORE : There'd be some real competition there to keep us honest and growing. This town doesn't have any challenges for the likes of us.

SUN RA : I like the way you're thinking. We might even recruit some new members from all those jazzers in New York. We could really take a bite of that apple.

ALTON ABRAHAM : A new city for a new decade! The sixties could be your time, Sun Ra.

MARSHALL ALLEN : And New York could be your place.

SUN RA : Space is my place. But New York might help get me there better then Birmingham or Chicago did. The space aliens told me I had a special destiny. But I have to nurture it, not just coast.

JOHN GILMORE : Ronnie Boykins' dad has a big station wagon we can take that'll hold our traveling instruments and us.

SUN RA : Well sure. And we can always go back to Chicago if we can't cut it in New York.

ALTON ABRAHAM : But you will. You know you're that good.

JOHN GILMORE : The best!

SUN RA : From what I've heard, New York could use some discipline.

MARSHALL ALLEN : Let's call that booking agent and start packing!

Fade to black.

End act one.

Act Two

Concessions continue to be sold and/or given away in the lobby. When the audience returns to the theatre, though, the stage is dark and there is no music playing. The lights come up on a bar, Slug's, New York's lower east side, late 1960s, suitably decorated with period effects and beer signs. A bar and barstools should be on stage left. Various counterculture types, colorfully dressed (but not as colorfully as THE ARKESTRA!) are mingling and muttering at the bar. The director can have fun here, like having one of the barflies look like Bob Dylan when he had big hair. There is a band stand and instruments set up in the back of the rest of the stage.

More importantly, there are two Saturn aliens at the bar, DREXEL and RORRG. They're a bit disheveled, having spent too much time on this planet monitoring SUN RA's progress. (Maybe bend their antennae?)

Scene 1: New York, Slug's, 1969

DREXEL : Hey bartender, how about some service?

   The caucasian bartender steps up.

BARTENDER : Sure. What'll you have?

   Pause.

BARTENDER : Say, you're not from around here, are you?

RORRG : No, we're from Brooklyn.

   Both ALIENS laugh.

DREXEL : Hey, you got any Sweet Lucy?

RORRG : Or how about some White Girl?

BARTENDER : What are you guys talking about?

DREXEL : Nothing, ofay. I guess we'll just be drinking wine spo-de-odee tonight.

Pause.

DREXEL : Naw, fuck it. Just give us a couple of Rolling Rocks.

BARTENDER : You got it. Coming right up.

RORRG turns to the BARFLY sitting next to him. Maybe it's the Dylan BARFLY if so desired.

RORRG : So what do you think of this shit so far?

BARFLY : What shit? The concert? The revolution?

RORRG : The play, motherfucker. You're in a play.

BARFLY : I am?

RORRG : Yeah, you are— and so far it's a damn shitty one.

The BARFLY looks confused.

BARFLY : Are you guys stoned?

RORRG : Not yet, but we're trying to get there. Are you holding?

DREXEL joins the conversation.

DREXEL : You know why this play sucks? It's got no sustained conflict. Motherfucker who wrote it should have read his Aristotle.

BARFLY : You guys are fucking with me, right?

RORRG : No, we're serious as cancer.

DREXEL : We're serious as two heart attacks. You're in a play.

The BARTENDER brings them their Rolling Rocks.

BARTENDER : Here you go, gentlemen.

They pay for the beers.

RORRG : I think the reason why there's no conflict is that the author likes Sun Ra too much. He saw him ten years and change from now at a club that will open in Washington called D.C. Space with his friends Ken Watson and Tom Silverstein. They were all on acid. The guy who wrote this was wearing a space helmet and a cape. When Ra came on stage, Ra looked through him with his burning eyes and converted him instantly to the space religion. Nothing good can come of that!

DREXEL : Certainly no decent art, as you can see!

Act II.i

RORRG : Plus, what do you want? He's a fucking honkie like you.

BARFLY : How do you guys know about stuff in the future which leads us to be in a play set in the past?

DREXEL : It's simple. We can bend space AND time AND reality, bitch!

RORRG : Can you dig it?

BARFLY : No man, I'm too mellow. I'm just here to check out the band.

> *The BARFLY vacates his stool. A man in a suit who can either enter the scene or shift his seat elsewhere at the bar comes up and takes the barfly's place. He works for NASA.*

NASA OFFICIAL : Greetings, gentlemen. Or should I say "Klaatu Barada Nikto"?

DREXEL : Hey, we're not fucking Masons.

NASA OFFICIAL : Well, you sure look like it. I'll buy your next round. You see, I need your help.

RORRG : So does this whole planet, if you know what I mean—and I think you do.

NASA OFFICIAL : Yeah, I've been tailing you guys just like you've been tailing Mister Sun Ra.

> *Pause.*

NASA OFFICIAL : I'll cut to the chase. I work for the National Aeronautics and Space Administration and we've been aware of some unusual, shall we say, "activity" since the Air Force more or less shut down Project Blue Book by defunding it. And now we have a little problem down in Florida that needs, shall we say, an outside opinion.

DREXEL : So your government is coming to us after telling everybody we don't exist.

RORRG : That's fucking whack. You owe us two beers and a couple of shots of tequila. That's the lowest consulting fee we can offer you after all the shit you people have pulled. Why'd you stop us from easing into contact with you mutts?

NASA OFFICIAL : You saw *2001*, right? It's like that. Our exo-sociologists feared culture shock, like what happened to the Native Americans when the Europeans arrived.

DREXEL : And whose shit was that, Big Suit?

NASA OFFICIAL : I know, I know. Water under the bridge—and lessons learned.

RORRG : Blood under the bridge, motherfucker!

DREXEL : And that shit you pulled at Roswell.

Pause.

DREXEL : Just kidding. We know that was Joseph Stalin using captured Nazi scientists to fuck with you.

Both laugh.

NASA OFFICIAL : You guys are very well-informed. Maybe you even know about what's going on in Florida?

RORRG : Naw, we're not like those aliens in *2001*. We're not omniscient or anything.

DREXEL : But we're pretty good. Set up some beers and tequila and we'll talk.

The NASA OFFICIAL beckons to the BARTENDER and gives the order.

NASA OFFICIAL : Okay, here's the nut. Ever since the moon landing, there's been something happening to the people around the launch pad at Cape Kennedy which we call the "space sickness." The symptoms are very simple. People are sleeping incrementally a bit more each day, just five minutes more per day. But it adds up. We started worrying when some residents got up to thirteen, fourteen hours. And it's spreading about a city block a day from the launch pad. The symptoms are now found as far away as Cocoa Beach and beyond all along the Space Coast. In time it will hit Orlando if we don't do something about it. You guys know anything about this?

The drinks arrive.

DREXEL : It's not our posse's doing, that's for sure.

RORRG : We're more into non-lethal weapons that fire chewing gum.

Both laugh.

NASA OFFICIAL : So far we've kept a media blackout more or less. Older people sometimes sleep more, after all. And we've let people think that perhaps some tse-tse flies are causing sleeping sickness. But we can't keep this up forever. The symptoms are different. There's no fever at all, just a gradual inability to stay awake. And the progression is mathematical almost—a clearly measurable time unit. Same for everybody.

DREXEL : Does this have anything to do with the shit you brought back from the moon?

Act II.i

NASA OFFICIAL : No. This is emanating in concentric circles from the launch pad, not from where the moon rocks are kept. Oh, and by the way, it only affects humans. Fishes, birds, cats and dogs aren't affected.

Pause.

NASA OFFICIAL : Now we get to the really weird stuff. Two things: first, no one – and I mean no one—working for NASA in any capacity has caught the "illness."

He makes quotation marks with his hands.

NASA OFFICIAL : We're all immune, right down to the catering service that feeds us. Even the bartenders who serve the astronauts drinks. Anyone connected to NASA at all in any way is immune.

RORRG : Whoa, I can see why you suspected us. That sounds like an intelligent action, not a random disease.

NASA OFFICIAL : Exactly. And here's the second weird thing, the other category of people that seem to be immune to the syndrome. We first noticed it when we heard this strange music coming out of a stereo system in a neighborhood otherwise dozing away from the space sickness. Can you guess what it was?

DREXEL : Yoko Ono?

RORRG : Frank Zappa? They're real big on our home world.

NASA OFFICIAL : Our investigators came in under some pretext, feigned curiosity I guess, and found the album playing was *Cosmic Tones for Mental Therapy* by Sun Ra.

RORRG : I'll be damned.

NASA OFFICIAL : Yep. And it turns out that every house that had a Sun Ra album in it that we found—not that we were doing massive searches—was immune. Record stores that carry his stuff were; ones that didn't weren't.

Pause.

NASA OFFICIAL : So you see, gentlemen, we need your help—and quite probably Sun Ra's. We have a big mystery down there with very peculiar leads. And that's why I'm at this concert. I need information.

Pause.

NASA OFFICIAL : Can you get us backstage?

RORRG : Sure, but that's no big deal. Sun Ra likes to talk to people about his beliefs.

DREXEL : Anyone can see him after the show.

RORRG : But fair warning. He pretty much plays almost all night long. The thing is he hardly ever sleeps.

NASA OFFICIAL : No problem. This is way too important. I'll just switch to coffee at some point.

DREXEL : You might be better off with Coke. The coffee here leaves a lot to be desired.

> THE ARKESTRA files in from stage right with their flamboyant costumes. DREXEL, RORRG and the NASA OFFICIAL remain at the bar drinking and listening. A few percussionists should come in first and start laying down some polyrhythms. It is apparent that the group has gotten bigger. There are three female DANCERS, including JUNE TYSON. The DANCERS should be dressed wildly, but in ways that will not restrict their movements. Everyone in the band is African American, of course.
>
> JUNE TYSON and SUN RA process up to a microphone at the front of the stage. He makes a brief nod in the direction of DREXEL and RORRG.

SUN RA AND JUNE TYSON : It's after the end of the world. Don't you know that yet?

JUNE TYSON : It's after the end of the world. Don't you know that yet?

SUN RA AND JUNE TYSON : It's after the end of the world. Don't you know that yet?

> PAT PATRICK steps up and plays an extended baritone saxophone solo of a highly "free" and atonal nature, randomly playing runs and pushing the reed to the breaking point. This can be mimed to tape if the musician is incapable of delivering such a performance.
>
> Either way this will be a hard part of the scene to stage, as it is the most thoroughly music-driven. Whether the band plays this challenging material or mimes to a pit orchestra or a tape, lots of practice will be needed. Video footage of the actual ARKESTRA should be consulted for tips!
>
> Bar patrons should respond enthusiastically. If the bar is sturdy enough. the players may jump on it.
>
> This is followed by MARSHALL ALLEN, doing the same on an alto sax; then by JOHN GILMORE on tenor.

> *When he is finished, the band plays (or fakes) the introductory riff from "Shadow World."*
>
> *This in turn transitions into the lead melody of "Watusa," followed by an extensive and furious percussion and drum improvisation. The DANCERS swirl to it, striking ancient Egyptian hieroglyphic poses. They may go into the aisles of the theater if so desired.*
>
> *After about ten minutes of drumming, things get quieter and softer. One male ARKESTRA MEMBER prowls the front of the stage, hand above his eyes, peering into the audience.*

ARKESTRA MEMBER : What planet is this? What planet is THIS?

OTHER MEMBERS OF THE ARKESTRA : Calling Planet Earth! Calling Planet Earth!

> *The volume of the percussion increases and the main theme of "Watusa" is restated. When the song stops, bar patrons applaud enthusiastically as stage lights fade to black. Some of SUN RA's synthesizer solo music should play while the set is changed.*
>
> *Lights come up on a rehearsal space in the Morton Street House of Ra in Philadelphia, about a month later than the previous scene. The set can look fairly similar to the Chicago apartment in the first act. Again, there is a piano. SUN RA, JOHN GILMORE, MARSHALL ALLEN, JAMES JACSON and OTHER MEMBERS OF THE ARKESTRA are hanging around between rehearsal performances.*

Scene 2: Philadelphia, House of Ra, 1969

MARSHALL ALLEN : It's good to be back at the house. Did you hear what happened to Verta Mae last week?

JOHN GILMORE : No.

MARSHALL ALLEN : After the last set at Slug's, she went over to an all-night store to buy some milk for her kid's cereal and some drugged-out guy who had been at the show saw her and freaked out. He yelled out "You ain't going nowhere, space bitch!"—or words to that effect—and tried to get the clerk to help him capture the alien in their midst.

> *Nervous laughter.*

JOHN GILMORE : Our show and those psychedelic drugs are a pretty heady mix. People really believe we all are from outer space, and they don't always dig it.

SUN RA : Now you know some of us are from other worlds.

JOHN GILMORE : I know, Sonny. But I know I'm not.

SUN RA : Still, I'm getting you ready to go to outer space with me. Meanwhile, here's something a little more down to Earth for you.

He plays a simple piano vamp.

SUN RA :

When you eat, don't eat too fast
Or you'll make music with your ass

He repeats the riff and vocal for a while. OTHER MEMBERS OF THE ARKESTRA sing along, clap along, make farting noises in time to the music and interject nonsense syllables like "beep beep." All eventually break down in laughter.

SUN RA : So what do you think, Honest John? Do we have a hit single here?

JOHN GILMORE : I got to give it to you boss, it's pretty catchy.

SUN RA : The other one I've been working on is that old Charles Bates tune, "Hard Hearted Hannah."

He plays that vamp.

SUN RA :

I saw hard hearted Hannah on the seashore with a great big fan
I saw hard hearted Hannah on the seashore with a great big fan
I saw hard hearted Hannah trying to pour some water on a drowning man
I saw hard hearted Hannah trying to pour some water on a drowning man

He repeats the verse three times; THE ARKESTRA joins in on the vocals.

SUN RA :

Hard hearted Hannah just love to see men suffer
Hard hearted Hannah just love to see men suffer
Life is tough, but with hard hearted Hannah it's tougher.
Life is tough, but with hard hearted Hannah it's tougher.

Act II.ii

Again, he repeats the verse and THE ARKESTRA joins in.

SUN RA : You know, they say the dead are rising in Jersey and I believe that. Once when I was in Chicago, I met a man who smelled just like he come out of the grave. He was on a bus. He had that smell like mildew. Like he was just out of the grave. I met a girl in Paris who smelled like that too.

JOHN GILMORE : Remember that green man we met once? He was real green head to toe and it wasn't paint.

SUN RA : You better get some spiritual wisdom in case you meet one of those dead ones.

Pause.

SUN RA : I had a member of the band who told me he died in Casablanca. He told his parents and me. "Sun Ra," he said. "I died."

Pause.

SUN RA : The phone's going to ring. Somebody better answer it.

MARSHALL ALLEN walks over to phone and picks it up before it rings.

MARSHALL ALLEN : You have reached outer space ... . Yeah that's right. He's here. Just a minute. May I ask who's calling?

Pause.

MARSHALL ALLEN : Sun Ra, it's for you. It's that guy from NASA we met backstage last month at Slug's. He wants to hire us for a concert in Orlando, Florida.

SUN RA walks over to the phone and takes it from MARSHALL ALLEN.

SUN RA : Yeah, we're interested. We talked about expenses, right? Travel, hotels, food, up-front cash and a percentage of the gate?

Pause.

SUN RA : Could you send that to us as a money order? We're going to need that up-front cash to travel down there. We have our own cars, but we have to put gas in them.

Pause.

SUN RA : That sounds good. I'll call you at that number if there's any problems with the money order. Otherwise, we should be down there in plenty of time for the show. We like playing open air venues. It's easier for the UFOs to hear us. See you then.

SUN RA hangs up and walks over to the rest of the band.

SUN RA : Well that's the damndest thing. We've never been hired by NASA before.

MARSHALL ALLEN : Why do they want us?

SUN RA : Well, that guy sure wasn't going to tell us. But those two aliens he was with told me something after he left. In strictest confidence, but they don't worry about us. Who's going to believe us if we do talk?

Laughter.

SUN RA : It seems there's some kind of sleeping sickness down there which affects everybody except people who work for NASA and folks who listen to us. The symptoms are that you just keep sleeping more each day until you never get up. They're paying us all this money for the concert because they want us to stop the spread of the disease, to inoculate the listeners.

JOHN GILMORE : That's pretty far out.

SUN RA : The odd thing is that those aliens said they didn't know anything about the so-called "space sickness." It's not coming from them or any alien civilizations they're monitoring.

PAT PATRICK : So who's behind this? The Russians?

SUN RA : I don't think so. Those aliens dropped some broad hints that they might be having trouble with this over there as well.

Pause.

SUN RA : Here's what I've been thinking. What do NASA and the band have in common? And in whose interest would it be to encourage people connected to us or the space program, but only those people? Nobody else. Y'all think about those two questions and see what answers you come up with.

Long pause.

JAMES JACSON : Well, both NASA and the Arkestra are encouraging people to leave Earth ... .

SUN RA : Exactly. And who would want humans to depart from the planet? There's your smoking gun.

Long pause.

JOHN GILMORE : They talk about Mother Earth. Maybe Earth is a conscious being and fed up with all the mess we're making with the environment and atomic bombs. So her immune system is kicking in,

Act II.iii 75

and saying "leave or die." And that sleeping sickness is a gentle way to do it.

SUN RA : That's a good theory.

MARSHALL ALLEN : Or maybe it's like in that movie we saw, *2001*. Extremely advanced aliens might have helped us develop here, but now they want us to go further out into the cosmos and meet them. So they programmed this sickness to kick in at a certain time in our development to goad us into the next step of the space age. Or maybe they just sent the sickness to us in a meteor or something after they saw we landed on the moon and were ready to proceed.

SUN RA : I like that idea, too. And there might be other explanations as well. I told you guys about Richard Shaver, that man in the fifties who discovered that ancient alien civilization living under the Earth. There might be beings down there who want us to leave so they can settle up here. Maybe they're tired of that cold and damp. The Dero, he calls them, got machines down there that can do all kinds of stuff. Why couldn't they spread this illness?

> *Pause.*

SUN RA : Despite what John said earlier, we don't know where the human race came from. Earth is not necessarily their place of origin. They might have crashed here, or been placed here. Now they got to find their true home.

PAT PATRICK : And there are probably lots of beings waiting for us to leave. Not just those Deros you were talking about, but leprechauns and gremlins and fairies and elves and other alien races among us.

SUN RA : When we play this concert, maybe they'll tip their hat.

> *Lights black out. The SUN RA composition "Planet Earth" plays while the set is changed to a musical stage like we had at the opening of the play. We are tacitly in Orlando, Florida. Lights come up on the end of the piece which they might be playing or playing along with.*

Scene 3: Orlando, 1969

> *After applause (recorded or encouraged by plants in the audience), they break into "Space Is the Place."*

SUN RA :

> Space is the place
> Space is the place
> Space is the place, yeah
> Space is the place

JUNE TYSON :

> There's no limit to the things that you can do
> There's no limit to the places you can be
> Your thought is free
> And your life is worthwhile

THE ARKESTRA : Space is the place!

> *The musical vamp gradually fades to accompanying percussion, which will be the only instrumental music for the rest of the scene. From the back of the room, cheap lasers play over the heads of the audience from the ALIENS (including DREXEL and RORRG) as they march down the aisle and join the band on-stage.*

ALIENS IN UNISON : We are the astro nation of the united planets of the omniverse

> We are the astro nation of the united planets of the omniverse (*repeat until they arrive on stage*)

SUN RA : Prepare yourself for the journey to other worlds
You better get ready to leave Earth

> *A giant puppet of MOTHER EARTH/GAIA comes on stage from the side. (In the Caribbean they call these "mocko jumbies.")*

MOTHER EARTH/GAIA : Earthmen out of the pool! NOW!

> *The PUPPET continues swaying along with the space chants. So do the ALIENS.*

SUN RA :

> If you find Earth boring
> Just the same old same thing
> Come and sign up
> To Outer Spaceways, Incorporated

> (*2 times, second accompanied by THE ARKESTRA*)

SUN RA : Rocket number nine, take off for the planet Venus

THE ARKESTRA : Venus! Venus!

Act II.iii 77

SUN RA : Rocket number nine, take off for the planet Venus

THE ARKESTRA : Venus! Venus!

SUN RA : Zoom! Zoom! Up, up in the air!

THE ARKESTRA : Zoom! Zoom! Up, up in the air!

SUN RA : The second stop is Jupiter

THE ARKESTRA (robotically):

>The second stop is Jupiter
>The second stop is Jupiter

SUN RA : Why go to the moon? Try Pluto too!

THE ARKESTRA : Pluto too! Pluto too!

SUN RA : Try Venus!

THE ARKESTRA : Try Venus!

SUN RA : Try Neptune!

THE ARKESTRA : Try Neptune!

SUNRA AND THE ARKESTRA : Have you heard the news from Neptune, Neptune, Neptune? Have you heard the news from Neptune, Neptune, Neptune?

SUN RA : Try Saturn!

THE ARKESTRA : Try Saturn!

SUN RA :

>Saturn is the planet of discipline
>Saturn is the great taskmaster

THE ARKESTRA : Saturn rings, rings around Saturn (*4 times*)

>*The ALIENS shoot silly string into the audience. Ed Wood painted flying saucer plates drop down on strings above the stage.*

THE ARKESTRA :

>Little Sally Walker
>Sitting in a saucer
>What kind of saucer?
>A flying saucer!
>
>(*2 times*)

SUNRA AND THE ARKESTRA :

Interplanetary, interplanetary, interplanetary music
Interplanetary melodies
Interplanetary harmonies
Interplanetary, interplanetary, interplanetary music

We travel the spaceways
From planet to planet

As they keep chanting these last two lines, SUN RA and THE ARKESTRA leave the stage and march down the aisles and out of the theatre. Only the percussionists, ALIENS and MOTHER EARTH/GAIA remain on stage. After THE ARKESTRA has left and the chant fades from hearing, the ALIENS start their exit chant.

ALIENS IN UNISON :

We're traveling
A strange celestial road
A strange celestial road
To endless ever

As they keep repeating this chant, they march down the aisles and out of the theatre. They may shoot more silly string at the audience as they process. Only MOTHER EARTH/GAIA and the percussionists remain on stage. The beat stops.

Blackout and curtain.

Notes for the Play

The idea for this play came from a realization that for the twentieth anniversary of his departure from planet Earth, Sun Ra needed a theatrical memorial as well as his touring ghost band (which will not be able to continue forever, probably, given its aging members) and the record on audio and video. I'd aleady done the research for the Sun Ra chapter in *Adventures in Avant Pop* (Naciketas Press, 2013)—updated in this book—and I wanted it to come alive. Although I have invented most of the dialogue, the space chants are from actual recordings by the Arkestra. Producers of this play should try to get in touch with living members of the band and pay some negotiated royalties. This is a history play, and it unabashedly appropriates pre-existing materials—for accuracy, not profit.

A director might well want to seek the source materials for these chants to get the melodies right. Most of them can be found on the massive *Detroit Jazz Center Residency* box set from Transparency. The "Sin" monologue comes from Transparency's *Audio Series* Volume Two, *Live at the Club Lingerie in Hollywood*. The songs in Act Two, Scene Two are on Transparency's *Lost Reel Collection*, Volume Four (*Dance of the Living Image*). In the text of the play I have given sources for some other material.

The best version of "Discipline 27-II" I'd point a director to can be found on *The Universe Sent Me, Transparency's Lost Reel Collection* Volume Five. It's an early instrumental reading of the piece without the typical declamations recited over it; as such, it's a good blank canvas recording to talk over. Jazz bassist Bill McKemy in Kansas City is willing to transcribe it for performance. Contact him at 816-582-5065 or on his website if you'd like him to do this.

The "space sickness" plot development is borrowed from several short stories by J.G. Ballard collected in *Myths of the Near Future*, paying tribute to another deceased genius interpreter of the space age.

Anyone writing about Sun Ra stands in the shadow of John Szwed, whose biography *Space Is the Place* remains the single best book about this cosmic being.

Discipline 27-II did get produced in St. Louis in April of 2015 at Forest Park Community College. Its abundance of good roles for African Americans was a strong selling point.

Let me conclude these remarks by talking about what I learned from those four performances of *Discipline 27-II* (a Thursday matinee, evening Friday and Saturday shows and a Sunday matinee), expertly directed by my former Truman colleague Mary Hurley (who has gone on to other good thespian endeavors in California since). One performance was filmed by videogapher Protein Williams, making it possible for me to re-view, to focus on how it came across. Overall, it played well. A largely African American audience laughed a lot at the humor and even made some call-and-response vocalizations when something in the play hit home. The latter was beyond my wildest expectations. And most folks seem surprised to find out that I had written it, even though I outed my ethnic identity in the first scene in Act Two. I also took that as a compliment.

Ms. Hurley made some changes in the production which are worth relaying to future directors of this play, at least for consideration. She changed my historical use of the "n-word" to "boy" when it came up in the racist judge's talk: a perfectly viable and less volatile substitution others may wish to emulate. She also brilliantly worked in references to the recent troubles in Ferguson, Missouri at the play's climax. When the aliens were firing silly string, only half did so while the others raised their hands in highly theatrical "hands up, don't shoot" gestures in the broad style of jazzbos in Tex Avery cartoons. Unfortunately, given the state of our world for the foreseeable future, references to current events involving racial conflict may be readily worked into productions of the play as needed / desired.

And as a result of these performances, I made a change in the script from what was performed. The reference to Norman Mailer in the first act drew a complete blank response from every audience who saw the production. (Lo, how are the mighty fallen!) By the fourth performance, the actor who played the narrating alien just delivered the line for laughs: I know you don't know who this is, but I have to say this dumb line! In this revision, I have turned the moment into an historical trivia contest that breaks the fourth wall. Let's see if this works: I do want to keep the line because it's an interesting example of the powers of Sun Ra's space music. This anecdote really happened!

Future directors are encouraged to do whatever they think needs to be done to make the play work for their production. And if you do decide to perform this play, let my publisher know via an e-mail to his website. I don't want to charge any fees for a performance (although I'd encourage donations to appropriate charities if there is any money to spare), but I'd like to hear how the shows went. Who knows? Directors and actors might inspire me to make future revisions to these texts on the basis of their discoveries.

Finally, I'd like to dedicate this play to my late friend Ken Watson, who shared with me many experiences of listening to this material and other amazing jazz. He is sorely missed by many.

Part III
Critical Remarks

Transition

You've now gotten another take on Sun Ra from a dramatic perspective. Had enough, or ready for more? (Or split the difference and take a break from reading — as long as necessary.)

What follows next is the portion of the Sun Ra critical chapter in **Adventures in Avant-Pop** *(2013) that offers a pretty comprehensive, even exhaustive (exhausting?!) listening and viewing guide to Sun Ra's music in the studio and in performance. Depending on your level of interest, you might want to read every word I wrote, dip into the particular phases of his career or the kinds of music he made that interest you most, or just skim the lot until something intrigues. Whatever works best!*

The original chapter's ending, included here, made as well a foray into addressing the project of Sun Ra's poetry, and "Why Sun Ra Matters." Since this material is six years old, I will conclude this book with a new global update of the highlights of what has come since — especially addressing additional Ra resources on streaming services such as Spotify and YouTube. I will also briefly discuss the insights contained in the newest major Ra scholarship, especially Paul Youngquist's **A Pure Solar World: Sun Ra and the Birth of Afrofuturism** *(University of Texas Press, 2016). I find Youngquist's analysis of Sun Ra's space poetry far supercedes my own humble efforts. For this and other reasons, Youngquist's book belongs on the shelf alongside the other major Ra scholars (Szwed, Corbett, Campbell, etc.).*

The good news for any admirer of Sun Ra's music is that, as of 2019, the only Sun Ra release of some interest that is relatively unavailable is **Hidden Fire (Volume 2)**. **Hidden Fire (Volume 1)** *is available on YouTube at a click. The former is for sale on vinyl for $560.67 via the <discogs.com> website — several copies, in fact, shipping from Germany. Too rich an expenditure for this author! I sincerely hope that this material will in time also become available in a more financially accessible format. But the good news is that everything else one could possibly want to listen to by Sun Ra — and more! — is readily at hand. For this state of affairs, many individuals deserve our thanks: Marshall Allen and all the major scholars and archivists of the Ra legacy named or to be named, for starters.*

You can dive as deeply into this challenging and sublime ouevre as you wish. I obviously believe it repays every existential second you offer to it... .

Some Omniversal Listening Suggestions

For several reasons, I am not going to proceed with a ranking of Ra's recordings. The most practical one is that only a handful of people—and I am not one of them—have them all. The Saturn releases were too obscure and backdoor an operation for gaps not to appear in the most ardent Ra collector's holdings. As it is, I will be referring here to many releases which you will only be able to obtain at the most serendipitous of yard / estate sales, off e-bay or at a vintage vinyl store (in the latter two cases, at exorbitant prices). The good news is that much first-rate Sun Ra is available easily, and more is being made available as we speak—largely due initially to the Evidence label in Pennsylvania, which contracted to undertake massive reissues of the original Saturn recordings. Other labels have since come on board with both old and previously unissued Ra music: John Corbett's Unheard Music series, Leo records, Art Yard and Transparency.

A second reason for less thoroughness is the reduced status of the recorded artifact for Sun Ra. There are reasons for this tied in with African-American and jazz aesthetic preferences. Like James Brown, Ra eschewed Euro-American linearity and progression in favor of repetition and circularity (Rose 120). Arkestra trumpeter Lucious Randolph describes this proclivity on the level of the individual composition:

> Sonny gave his drummers long solos ... and sometimes asked them to play the same thing over and over until you could hear something else in it. You'd ask him, "How long is this going to go on?" and Sonny would answer, "I'm trying to tell you something else ... like, if you keep eating peach pie every day, [sooner or later] it's going to taste like something else." (Szwed 144)

Ra's career was cyclic on the macroscopic level as well. The classic Ra show (as it certainly developed by the mid-seventies) had a circular structure as well: an invocation of Ra by the band and June Tyson, ecstatic soloing by the Arkestra to scare off the musically timid, a space sermon from Ra like "I, Pharaoh" or "Discipline 27-II" (optional—if Sun Ra was in a good mood), a blend of jazz classics (from Fletcher Henderson, Todd Dameron, Duke Ellington and even Thelonious Monk and Miles Davis) and classic Ra compositions ("Lights on a Satellite," "Fate in a Pleasant Mood"), closing space chants and a prolonged exit involving the band circling through the audience, offstage and onstage again (usually to the tune of "We Travel the Spaceways" or "Space Is the Place"). In other words, the shows began and ended with the space material framing a more conventional jazz concert. And then on to the next gig. This is not to deny that Ra introduced variations into this outline, but to suggest that there was a basic structure. You can hear it quite clearly on the 1976 recording *Live at Montreux* or 1983's *Love in Outer Space: Live in Utrecht*—or any of the more documentary-like recordings of live performances.

Larger cycles in the career included his occasional emphases upon synthesizers, organ or solo piano. At certain times he would get into a groove relying upon one of these instruments especially for awhile, give it up more or less, and then return to it. This can be heard when you listen to the recordings chronologically. And Ra's biggest cyclic act was to record shortly before his death a tribute to Stuff Smith, the violinist he played with on his earliest recording "Deep Purple." On this later session, he even re-recorded it. Sun Ra had come full circle.

This sense of a long project unfolding, combined with a tendency to privilege live performance, meant that Ra had less fetishistic regard for the recording process or its results. Saturn recordings are markedly casual: one hears tape recorders being turned on, phones ringing in the background, abrupt starts and stops. The idea of producing a concept album that would take the listener on a narrative journey was alien to Ra; the records were audio souvenirs of live musical events. One finds a similar attitude in James Brown's recorded work. James thought more on the level of the individual studio track than the album, which is why only his live albums (like some of Ra's) have a feeling of development at all (circular though they might be, live shows at least have to end!). Neither Ra nor Brown gave us a *Sergeant Pepper*—or wanted to. It would take a later African-American artist like Prince to want to attempt such a development (especially on *The Rainbow Children*).

All by way of saying that Sun Ra's recordings merit discussion more for the quality of the songs on them than the albums as conceptual wholes. The best releases contain a critical mass of superb material, but overall Ra beckons the collector to shuffle the material onto customized mix tapes.

As with Frank Zappa, all of Ra's music is extraordinary. The gap between his "best" stuff and his least interesting material is small, so one personally negotiates to what extent Sun Ra is a musical seasoning in a record / CD collection or a source of fetishistic pursuit. I don't think one can own just a single Sun Ra recording (Evidence's greatest hits single CD is ultimately a genial in-joke directed at real Arkestra aficionados). Since you can't own them all, let me point to what I think are some landmark recorded musical moments, arranged chronologically to show the band's development.

The Chicago Years (1948 - 1960)

Sound Sun Pleasure!! (1958, reissued by Evidence in 1991) is a good place to start any Ra listening voyage. It contains his earliest "Sun Ra" recordings as bonus tracks. I have already referred several times to "Deep Purple" with Stuff Smith; the vocal ballad "Dreams Come True" is also remarkable because of the gentle surrealism of its lyrics delivered by Clyde Williams (with a classic Billy Eckstine voicing). Off the original album, "Enlightenment " stands out as Ra's earliest standard. Destined to be performed throughout his long career, this jaunty tune (co-written with trumpeter Hobart Dotson) appears in its early instrumental guise. The lack of words in this early rendition is more than compensated for by the wild generic shifts in the presentation of the melody: now it's a cha-cha, now it's a march. Other highlights include "Back in Your Own Backyard," an ironically terrestrial sentiment for Ra, and a samba version of Lerner & Lowe's "I Could Have Danced All Night" that provides a showcase for the Arkestra's innovative use of flute textures (probably from Marshall Allen, but not credited as such). For Sun Ra, this is a very accessible and mainstream recording; but already the novice listener will detect a different approach to music than she has ever heard before.

Our next stop would be the *Sun Ra Visits Planet Earth / Interstellar Low Ways* twofer on Evidence (from 1957-1960 sessions). "Interplanetary Music" especially hits the main vein with Ronnie Boykins managing to make his bowed bass sound like a trumpet. The vocals for this song are beyond belief: doom-laden yet archly signifying space-age camp that you dare not laugh at. The Arkestra would do this for over three decades, but the tone is struck early here. "Interstellar Low Ways" is a lush mood piece for flute and soft percussion which also became a Ra standard.

In 1960, the last year the Arkestra was based in Chicago, several notable recording sessions were produced. *Fate in a Pleasant Mood* contains several Ra compositions destined to be revisited often over the years. The title track hits upon the major philosophical theme of changing your destiny (presumably to the alter-destiny) by finding fate in a pleasant mood. The various catchy riffs in the song could be extended in live rendition as long as desired; its conclusion often resulted in an Arkestral promenade around the performance space.

"Lights on a Satellite" from the same session shows the lush influence of Duke Ellington; its main flute melody mimics the spinning lights on the orbiting object. This composition is outer space program music perfectly in line with the zeitgeist of sputnik and Telstar. (I can recall going out at night in a much less polluted Milwaukee and being able to see these objects in the heavens—and wanting to see them as a great novelty!) Ronnie Boykins again delivers impressive arco bass. The piece's main theme resembles the alien melody enough in *Close Encounters of the Third Kind* (1977) to lead Ra admirers to suspect homage (or plagiarism) from Steven Spielberg / John Williams, but I fear it's just a happy coincidence. How sad, though, that the makers of science fiction films never realized what a goldmine these Ra compositions could have been as instant scores. I predict some day this oversight will be spectacularly rectified.

In typically mercurial fashion, Ra also recorded some jazz standards on the same day as his futuristic compositions, later released as *Holiday for Soul Dance*. The whole CD is wonderfully accessible, but a live recording of "Early Autumn" (from a slightly later gig that year) is nothing short of sublime because of Ricky Murray's dramatic vocals and John Gilmore's haunting tenor saxophone solo. Amidst the adventurous sonic exploration, Ra never forgets to remind you that he can be a better jazz traditionalist than those who never leave that idiom.

The New York Years (1961-1968)

Although Sun Ra and the Arkestra returned to New York City periodically for the rest of their respective lives to play live and make recordings, these eight years mark the extent of their actual residence in the Big Apple. They were appropriately based in the East Village, Alphabet City, at 48 East Third Street (Szwed 194). Paralleling the biography to the music, one could similarly note that although Ra made post-avant-garde gestures at least until the mid-1980s, the New York years marked the height of the band's experimentation. They equaled the musical events of those years, but they never surpassed them. Disciplined by a regular Monday night slot at Slug's tavern in the same area where they lived, the band developed a truly fierce energy which fortunately shows up even on the recordings. When drummer Tommy "Bugs" Hunter returned from Sweden and heard the Arkestra in 1965, he marveled that "It was like a fire storm coming off the bandstand" (Szwed 212).

You can hear this new attitude from the first recording made on the east coast, *The Futuristic Sounds of Sun Ra* (1961; Newark, New Jersey; on the Savoy label). The key moment of paradigm shift is on a track aptly entitled "The Beginning." (Like James Brown, who knew he was inventing a new genre when he called his first funk single "Papa's Got a Brand New Bag," Ra must have sensed the importance of the occasion.) "The Beginning" is an extended percussion experiment with fabulous guest congas contributed by Leah Ananda from Kashmir. It inaugurates a spatial approach to the music, a use of the band to create sonic landscapes rather than merely to play a melody and then offer solo variations on it (which, of course, Ra and the Arkestra always continued to do as well). There IS no melody discernible on this track, only rhythms and textures—a jazz equivalent of what Edgard Varese was doing in the 1920s as an avant-garde classicist. "The Beginning" offers a paradigm shift, and is the most important part of an overall wonderful session that features other fine tracks (including more vocals from Ricky Murray on "China Gate," the theme from the Sam Fuller film).

The following year brought several landmark recordings. *Art Forms of Dimensions Tomorrow* featured another experiment in sonic space, "The Outer Heavens." This composition has no drums, only a rhythmic piano accompanying reeds and trumpet. The music evokes floating bodies weightless in deep space, very reminiscent of Varese's turning crystalline sound structures. You can see this music if you let it take you where it wants to. Marshall Allen goes wild on alto sax; Ra's piano work demonstrates an energy that has led many jazz enthusiasts to compare him to Cecil Taylor (when he's in this mode of playing).

Secrets of the Sun (recorded in 1962, released in 1965) also finds Sun Ra and His Solar Arkestra (the name then) transitioning between the tight arrangements that characterized the Chicago years and the more open form explorations of the New York period. "Friendly Galaxy" and "Solar Differentials" are extraterrestrial versions of Les Baxter exotica (the latter highlighting "space bird sounds," Art Jenkins' "space voice" and reverb drenches from Tommy Hunter's tape recorder tricks). "Space Aura" is a piece originally from the Chicago days, but it is executed at "a psychotropically slow tempo" (as Ra scholar John Corbett accurately says in the liner notes to the CD reissue.

An early version of "Love in Outer Space" features John Gilmore wailing on bass clarinet for a change—and lots of "space drums." This piece would become a Ra standard whose gorgeous melody would be performed over the entire career; in later incarnations, it provided a showcase for extended Afrocentric drumming.

"Reflects Motion" offers a great showcase for Gilmore's more typical tenor saxophone and fine drum interplay between Tommy Hunter and C.

Scoby Stroman. "Solar Symbols" ends the original album with a pure percussion workout.

The CD adds a long bonus track "Flight to Mars," which was intended for the entire B side of an unreleased El Saturn long-player. It begins with a blast-off crescendo and Gilmore enthusing "all the way into space" before a tape edit transitions into stretched-out swinging and extended soloing from Marshall Allen on flute, Scoby Stroman on heavy drumming, Calvin Newborn on scintillating and subtle electric guitar and Ronnie Boykins bowing away on the upright bass. After seventeen minutes and thirty-five seconds of this solid groove, the tape abruptly ends. In length at least, this track presages wilder journeys to come.

The breakthrough recording of this year, however, is *When Sun Comes Out*. This is the first release where the experiments dominate the proceedings. "Circe" begins with big gongs played by Ra leading into Yma Sumac vocal stylings from Theda Barbara. (Ra's interest in Les Baxter is quite evident here.) "The Nile" provides more thick atmosphere with lots of percussion and Marshall Allen on flute. "Brazilian Sun" gives us Latin piano and percussion.

Then we leave our tour of the ancient world and head out into outer space! This journey is appropriately inaugurated with "We Travel the Spaceways," the space chant destined to close many an Arkestra concert. This is the definitive version, fully developed instrumentally and, as they say with a new meaning when applied to the Ra project, "far out." The soloing sure sounds free, even if it's scripted. "Calling Planet Earth" keeps up the pressure with echo-laden drums and Pat Patrick playing the baritone sax as if it's an alien message communicated to earthlings. The band plays slightly more conventionally on the next two tracks ("Dancing Shadows" and "The Rainmaker"), but the reed solos keep threatening to collapse the structures. "The Rainmaker" concludes with an early example of the space key / chord, a burst of noise worthy of the most discordant gestures of Charles Ives. The title track really cuts loose with outside horn work, piano played as a rhythm instrument with the drums, a squiggly Danny Davis alto solo and Walter Miller's trumpet on top of the proceedings. "Dimensions in Time" concludes this landmark session with John Gilmore playing a rare (and sporadically honking!) bass clarinet with the percussion section. The trajectory of the Arkestra's future experimentation was already cast as early as these 1962 recordings. What followed would extend their innovative discoveries.

Such is literally the case with "Next Stop Mars" off *When Angels Speak of Love* (1963). This track is the earliest in a series of sound sculptures long enough to fill the side of a long-playing album. It begins as a space chant, then proceeds to serious sonic experimentation: Cecil-Taylor-style piano from Ra, intense saxophone soloing by Allen (alto), Gilmore (tenor) and Pat Patrick (baritone).The solos are interspersed with wild echo effects produced by "Bugs" Hunter. He had discovered that he could achieve these results by recording with earphones on and running a cable from an output jack back into the input for the recorder. Without the headphones, only feedback would result; with the headphones on he could obtain massive reverb and control its speed by adjusting the volume on the tape recorder (Szwed 187). These effects made the music sound like it was being beamed into your stereo from a distant galaxy. "Next Stop Mars" was pre-psychedelic psychedelia.

In 1964, John Gilmore had a brief falling out with Sun Ra and the Arkestra. Immersed in the New York jazz scene, he thought he heard a lot of musicians stealing his ideas and making a lot more money when they played them in various venues. So he took a break from the group and toured Europe with Art Blakey's Jazz Messengers. It turned out that he had too big of an ego for Blakey to deal with, so he returned to the Arkestra in 1965 and stayed with the band for the rest of his life except for a few brief side projects (Szwed, *Space* 204-5, 213). This state of affairs led to Pharaoh Sanders, a much better known tenor saxophonist than Gilmore, joining the Arkestra. (Any Ra fan will tell you Gilmore is as good as or better than Sanders, but Pharaoh has more name recognition because of his distinguished solo career.)

The results of this realignment can be heard on *Sun Ra Featuring Pharaoh Sanders and Black Harold* (a flautist), an ESP Disk recording of a New Year's Eve 1964 concert at New York's Judson Hall (long unavailable on vinyl, but reissued in 2009 with 45 minutes of additional material). This is fabulous music, although one can tell that despite the brilliance of Pharaoh Sanders, Gilmore was a better fit for this band. Black Harold (Harold Murray) is arguably the more intriguing new sonic seasoning. On "The Now Tomorrow," his interplay with Sun Ra (playing piano and celeste at the same time)—later joined by Ronnie Boykins and Alan Silva (both on bass)—is remarkably nuanced and sensitive to the other musicians. When you add Art Jenkins' "space voice" to all of this. you have an improvised composition that is both wonderful and strange.[4] Jenkins also contributes spooky vocalese to "Discipline 9" (really a version of "We Travel The Spaceways"). "The Voice of Pan" offers more ethereal flute from Black Harold. When he intones into his flute some vocal stylings in the spirit of Rahsaan Roland Kirk (why should Jenkins have all the fun?), you can hear nervous laughter from the audience. This stuff sounds pretty unusual today; in late 1964, it was almost indescribable, as A. B. Spellman (the reviewer of the concert for *The Nation*) conceded: "how to render a sympathetic appraisal for what was one of the most exciting [concerts in the] series without making this group seem either utterly insane or sickeningly corny? ... well, you had to be there" (Szwed 206).

The Magic City (1965) continued Ra's experimentations, especially in its 27 minute title cut. This was collective improvisation, organized by hand signals to cue the individual Arkestra members to play certain prearranged sequences or effects (a method very similar to Frank Zappa's method of conducting). The result is musical freedom with a hidden structure. "The Magic City" was never performed in concert later: as John Gilmore said, it was "unreproducible, a tapestry of sound" (Szwed 214). Its title paid homage to the nickname of Birmingham, Alabama (Ra's terrestrial point of entry). But it also suggested an exotic realm of urban enchantment, closer to what you hear in the music. This piece sounds more like Samuel R. Delany's cities (in novels such as *Dhalgren*) than its ostensible referent. Still there is no doubt that Birmingham seen through the eyes of a youngster could be magical, especially if that child were Sun Ra.

The composition begins with the use of clavioline, a gentle electronic keyboard Ra favored at the time. A section of flutes come in imitating bird song. Gradually there is interplay among a baritone sax, arco bass and the clavioline; then more birdsong. John Gilmore and Danny Davis give reed solos of augmenting chaos, eventually joined by a whole saxophone ensemble simultaneously soloing. At around 24 minutes in, the sound thins to clavioline, piano and bass. At around 26:50, there is a final blast of the space key and a fade. You've been on an interesting journey and glimpsed a landscape, if not necessarily one in Dixie!

The Magic City recording also features "The Shadow World," a sporadic concert favorite with a torturously fast melody line for a bevy of saxes (its signature riff). The piece refers to Ra's quasi-Swedenborgian belief that other dimensions coexisted with ours. The spiritually attuned individual could catch glimpses of these other realms as shadows in our world. Ra also revealed that it's musically a serial composition deploying a twelve tone row (Szwed, liner notes for *The Magic City*). Ra's adaptation of Schoenberg's methods illustrates how far the band was moving from the sound of a jazz ensemble. Once in a guest lecture on modernism and postmodernism, I played an excerpt from the similarly adventurous "Atlantis" (see below). A room full of bright students took a very long time to guess its genre. They ventured jazz as an option after essaying classical and rock—only prior to country and western. To their ears, and that of many other listeners, Ra's music sounded like the farthest thing imaginable from jazz—especially as it is pumped out on digital music services. Like other composers such as Anthony Braxton, Sun Ra was beginning to create sound textures in a region somewhere between big-band jazz and twentieth-century avant-garde European classical. (For some of Ra's releases, you'd want to add a third musical lineage of sixties psychedelia achieved, like Zappa's, without the use of any chemicals.) *The Magic City*, and a few other releases of the years 1965-1968, offer clear aural evidence for this claim.

The Heliocentric Worlds of Sun Ra (Volumes 1 and 2) from 1965, for example, are avant-garde chamber jazz: a smaller version of the Arkestra playing meditative and complex compositions as close to Anton Webern as they are to Duke Ellington. The suitably named "Cosmic Chaos" off the second volume offers an early example of the reed battle royals that would constitute a significant portion of the Arkestra's music in performance and recorded legacy. Although Ra aficionados have their favorite examples of this routine, the sonic contours from one to the next are fairly consistent. The battle royals essentially consist of the reed section delivering highly athletic performances on their saxophones, soloing both serially and (sometimes) simultaneously. As good tone scientists, they use the saxophone in ways never imagined or intended by its developer: pushing the reed into making sounds at frequencies guaranteed to bother dogs, or using sustained circular breathing to keep the sound going. This rather free jazz in effect explored all the sounds one could get out of the sax. Its sonic vocabulary was not only extended but seemingly exhausted. I haven't heard any new ways to play it since the innovations of this decade.[5]

In May of 1966, Bernard Stollman arranged for the Arkestra to tour colleges in New York state with other avant-garde acts on his record label. Stollman was the owner of ESP Disk which Ra was now also recording for (the *Heliocentric Worlds* series) in addition to his own El Saturn releases. (ESP, by the way, refers to the invented Esperanto language—another Stollman interest—not extrasensory perception. Ra would have loved this linguistic serendipity, of course.) Forty minutes of one of the concerts at St. Lawrence University in Potsdam came out on ESP vinyl in 1969 as *Nothing Is* (Szwed, 237). In 2010, ninety additional minutes of the Potsdam shows came out on CD as *College Tour Volume I: The Complete Nothing Is ...* . (This numbering suggests more is to come!)

One of the highlights of the original release was "Exotic Forest," a loping percussion exploration augmented by Marshall Allen's North-African inflected oboe accompaniment. The result is an aural equivalent of Henri Rousseau's painting *The Dream* (which Ra had no doubt admired at New York's Museum of Modern Art). On this expanded version, there are many additional delights including a long, subdued take on "The Satellites Are Spinning" and two highly obscure piano-driven nonce pieces ("Nothing Is" [which was NOT on the original *Nothing Is*] and "Is Is Eternal"). The college audience is attentive and supportive: 1966 was truly a year poised to embrace any new cultural idea. On the cusp of the incrementally radical years that ended the decade, it seemed that ANYTHING was possible. You could walk from your dorm room into a concert hall and see black people from outer space wearing exotic costumes and blaring "Interplanetary Chaos" (an aptly titled improvisation on the expanded release).

The recent reissue of the hitherto rare *Strange Strings* set confirms that 1965-67 of the New York years showcased the most extreme experiments of an always-adventurous band (no date on the reissue, but the liner notes are dated 2006). I agree with Ra Scholar Hal Rammel that this 1966 recording should be linked with *The Magic City* (1965) and *Atlantis* (1967) as a trilogy of "master works" of epic proportions (liner notes, *Strange Strings*). The recording begins with "Worlds Approaching," an uncanny and atonal alien processional march, chock full of reverb and distortion. Ra even plays on a metal sculpture in homage to creators of sound sculpture such as Bernard and Francois Baschet, who were displaying their work at the Museum of Modern Art at the time. It is instructive to compare this piece with Zappa's processionals for the Grand Wazoo bands (including "Regyptian Strut"). Zappa sounds like muzak compared to this sublime feast reminiscent of more ominous and mysterious alien encounters like those in *2001* and *The Fifth Element*.

The aliens arrive in the remaining tracks. "Strings Strange" and "Strange Strange" are the result of Sun Ra's going to music stores and import shops in the city and buying up all manner of exotic stringed instruments—none of which his band knew how to play! They built a few more homemade ones as well, including sheet metal constructions that could produce thunderous noise. He called this "a study in ignorance." He was interested in the effect of highly trained musicians being put on a level playing field, all disadvantaged, with unfamiliar instruments. He was also thinking about how stringed instruments can emotionally affect listeners "in a special way" (Szwed, *Space* 237-8). He wanted to see if this communication could occur under these odd laboratory conditions with the aid of his aptly named "tone scientists" (often his preferred name for the musicians of the Arkestra).

The results? Hal Rammel tries to deliver program notes in the CD booklet, but I think there are some things language just can't accomplish. But I'll try: the truest statement is that this is like nothing you've ever heard before (or will hear since). It sounds like classical music from an alien civilization. Or, to be more banal, it evokes Sun Ra moving into the territory of Harry Partch—the maverick composer who built his own instruments (as here, mostly strings and percussion) and invented his own 32 note microtonal scale (because, yeah, exotic microtones abound). You know you're out there sonically when Arthur Jenkins' space vocals (lip-vibrating and "gargling" into various tubes and cylinders) are a reassuringly familiar strangeness (Rammel). At least we've heard this kind of oddity before in Ra's canon ... .

The surprise here is that this is not chaos. Ra is conducting them: structures and patterns emerge. These are improvised compositions, not mere noodling. Along with Ra's conducting, kudos should go to Clifford Jarvis on percussion and Ronnie Boykins on bass for laying down a focal groove for everything else to dance around. The results are sublime in the sense the Romantics intended, exactly the kind of sonic adventure I promised in the title of this book.

The reissue clinches the deal by an even more bizarre bonus track from the same sessions, "Door Squeak." This features Ra playing a squeaky door in the studio! He revels in its mix of gritty lows and high piercing tones, playing it like a "Mini-Moog" synthesizer (Rammel). Over the course of this ten-minute exploration, percussion and "strange strings" are eventually added to the piece. At this point in his musical development, Ra clearly felt almost anything was possible sonically. From a completely different background, he had come to embrace convictions similar to those of John Cage. (The difference, as oft noted, is that John became more minimalist as Ra became more maximalist.)

Then there's *Atlantis* (1967), the high-water mark (ouch) of the Arkestra's experimentalism. The major title work extends the discoveries of "Next Stop Mars" and "The Magic City" by fusing musical intensity with genuine program music. Apocalyptic program music, in fact, as Michael Shore asserts in the CD liner notes. You can hear the destruction of Atlantis conveyed through music. Given Ra's apocalyptic proclivities in interview, we are invited to read the fate of Atlantis as an allegory of what's in store for at least America, and most likely Planet Earth. As Ra told a French interviewer in 1984, we have to "turn or burn" (*Mystery, Mr. Ra*).

"Atlantis" begins, after a brief drum burst, with electronic keyboard beeps that various listeners have construed as either alarms or sonar pings probing the depths of the ocean in search of the lost city before flashing back to its destruction (the James Cameron reading of the composition). In either case, we transition into a highly theatrical keyboard meltdown on organ that certainly suggests massive sonic flooding. Eleven minutes into the piece Ra's Farfisa organ solo abruptly ends; at 11:30, a brooding French horn comes in. The keyboard returns soloing in a quieter fashion as if to offer a requiem for the initial catastrophe. At 13:30, the keyboard builds up again, giving us the aftershocks. At 15:30 a trombone comes in, followed by other horns playing a doom-laden theme. After 16:10, the horn section sounds exhausted by the crisis. (Ra discographer Robert Campbell has described this sound as the Arkestra doing Guy Lombardo [Shore, liner notes for *Atlantis*].) After 17:30, the keyboard returns for more electronic blasts, followed by percussion. The postmodern coup de grace happens at 21:25 when the Arkestra sings "Sun Ra, and his band, from outer space, have entertained you here": the apocalypse and/as show biz schtick. As the track fades, we hear the opening riff for a concluding "We Travel the Spaceways." This astonishing piece was recorded live at the Olatunji Center of African Culture, an utterly remarkable nonce event (Szwed 432).

The Transparency label has recently issued a double CD of the band live in early 1968 at New York's Electric Circus nightclub and at the Newport Jazz Festival in 1969 (after the move to Philadelphia). The sound quality is sub-standard, bootleg level (from audience tapes). But if you can overlook that deficiency, there is some interesting music on these discs. Newport reveals a version of "Shadow World" played at warp speed—the fastest reading of this lightning-paced piece that I've ever heard. The New York set has a 25 minute "untitled improvisation" with lots of electronic keyboard washes, and a reading of "Space Aura" that allows Gilmore to burn the zoo down with some wild soloing (to the amusement of the audience). As such, a fitting end to the highly formative New York years of the Arkestra.

The Philadelphia Years and the Arkestra on World Tour (1968-1992)

Studio Work (1968-1970)

In the fall of 1968, Sun Ra and the Arkestra moved into a row house in Philadelphia owned by Marshall Allen's father. Their East Village digs were drawing noise complaints from the neighbors, and the landlord was in the process of selling the property (Szwed 266). But who could have imagined that the house at 5626 Morton Street in the Germantown section of Philly would become the Arkestra's home for a quarter of a century (and beyond)? The band still played and recorded in New York on a regular basis—to say nothing of grueling global touring that took them all over the United States and to Mexico, Canada, Western and Eastern Europe, Russia, Egypt, Sub-Saharan Africa and Japan. But there was always a home base to come to, no matter how raggedy and dilapidated it might be at any given moment. For throughout this quarter century, there were never flush times. Although the perks for any given performance date could be flattering, the Arkestra's financial status was always in peril. Like Fletcher Henderson and Duke Ellington before him, Sun Ra learned how to keep a big band on the road—a miracle of economic and existential levitation.

These first years after the move were the time when Ra recorded *The Solar-Myth Approach (Volumes 1 and 2)*. I have already discussed the second volume, the first Ra recording I ever purchased, in the opening section of this book. Volume 1 contains "Seen III, Took 4." Along with "Scene 1, Take

1" off Volume 2 and the *My Brother the Wind* sessions (all 1969-1970), these are Ra's earliest recordings with Moog synthesizers. Like Edgard Varese before him, Ra was obsessed with the possibilities of the new electronic instruments duplicating potentially any sound. The synthesizer, however crudely, offered the promise of musical creation *ex nihilo*: if you could imagine it, you could program it and play it. These first recordings are humble efforts compared to what Ra could accomplish as the synthesizer itself expanded its capacities. (For instance, listen to the rich textures Ra could even get in live performance on a later recording such as *A Night in East Berlin* [1986].)

But Ra's synthesizer work has always been compelling. He used the synthesizer from the first as a sonic sketchpad to delineate his intergalactic visions. It was a bold accent in his concerts. He never tried to tame it like other jazz musicians such as Herbie Hancock and George Duke did. Although he could make it "swing," he never treated it as just another jazz keyboard to vamp on. Ra dared to outrage his audience with sublime celestial fire and thunder to a far greater extent than even psychedelic space-rock groups dared. (Nothing in Pink Floyd's or Hawkwind's catalogue matches the intensity of some of Ra's efforts.) If he risked leaving the jazz idiom altogether (although he was retaining its improvisatory aspect), so be it. Jazz was never more than a means to an end for Ra in any case.

My Brother the Wind, Volume 2 also features a few haunting Ra ballads. "Somebody Else's World" showcases June Tyson doing a modest version of Yma Sumac vocalese. Its lyrics are resolutely neoplatonic / Gnostic:

"Somebody else's idea of somebody else's world / Is not my idea of things as they are."

"Walking on the Moon" is a tribute to the Apollo 11 moon landing and a warning to black folks to get with the space age:

"If you wake up now / It won't be too soon."

One of Ra's baritone saxophonists contributes a sultry solo. (Danny Thompson? Or Pat Patrick? Information regarding personnel, let alone who's soloing, is typically sparse.)

Night of the Purple Moon (1970) is one of the best instrumental studio albums from the beginning of this era of the Arkestra, showcasing a return to a more concise approach to composition and a funkier aspect that would linger through the 1970s. Sun Ra was willing to engage the same issues as James Brown and Parliament / Funkadelic, albeit in his own distinctive manner. This outing also showcases a much smaller quartet version of the band: Sun Ra on keyboards (especially his new favorite, the gritty Roksichord [sic: the manufacturer called it a Rocksichord]); John Gilmore mostly on drums for a change; Danny Davis alternating among sax, clarinet, flute and more percussion; and Stafford James on electric bass. On the first side of the album (tracks 4-6 on the CD), Ra solos on two Mini-Moogs simultaneously with very sinuous and funky results.

The title track is light instrumental funk with a shimmering Roksichord keyboard leading the way. "A Bird's Eye View of Man's World" follows, emulating sudden aviary motions and offering wonderful bass work from Stafford James. "21st Century Romance" has a giant and insistent bass beat in the back and marvellous soloing by Danny Davis on alto. Then comes "Dance of the Living Image" with its way out bongo exotica and more Roksichord. The album concludes with a version of "Love in Outer Space" reinvigorated by alternate timbres: roksichord, Danny Davis' alto, jaunty percussion from John Gilmore and Danny Davis (doing double duty).

First European and African Tours (1970-1971)

The onset of the Arkestra's extensive touring in the early seventies led to the production of many live recordings. Some of these were issued contemporaneously; other sets, like the material in the vaults of activist / music promoter John Sinclair, have just shown up in the last few years as his personal affairs have begun to settle down. *Nuits de la Fondation Maeght, Volume 1* is the better half of a double release commemorating two August 1970 concerts in St.-Paul-de-Vence, France. This concert gives you a fine reading of Ra's classic "Enlightenment" and the lovely melody of "The Star Gazers." "The Shadow World" receives an intense workout with wild and sustained hocketing from the reed section and massive solos from everyone until blasts from the Moog and the space chord offer closure. "The Cosmic Explorer" is a long nonce Moog solo, augmented by percussion and Ra doing some doubling up on organ. He does indeed sound like he's exploring the cosmos in this engaging event.

Two later fall concerts in Germany from the same year have been collected on the double CD *Black Myth / Out in Space*. The latter disk is of special interest. The Arkestra typically began their concerts with group improvisation before settling into completely composed material. At 37 exuberant minutes, the opening title track from the Berlin show demonstrates how long they could keep this up without boring the sympathetic listener. It remains the longest and most thorough illustration of this facet of the Arkestra. This major piece opens with a chamber jazz segment; then African percussion and bass; a space chant assuring us that "Out in space is no disgrace"; a long series of uncompromising solos, including Ra turning his thunderous organ on and off for effect and playing a big Moog solo; and a final concluding space chord. Ra has talked about the effect his music can have on animals (liner notes, *Hours After*): this piece completely excites one of my cats! The rest of the set sustains this energy.

Of perhaps more historical / archival interest only (in other words, if you're becoming a diehard Ra fan) would be the November 9, 1970 UK debut of the Arkestra at Queen Elizabeth Hall in London (now available as a two-disc release from Transparency). The sound quality is that of an in-audience bootleg with lots of tape hiss. Its charms are largely ideological: the pounding percussion session of this massive touring ensemble talking back to the Empire! There is a lovely vocal rendition of "Planet Earth" in the second set, a full-tilt synthesizer buzz-out on "Myth vs. Reality"—and even a moment when the string section is getting sounds very akin to those heard on Gyorgy Ligeti's "Atmospheres." Even through the weak audio one can detect the utterly uncompromising nature of 1970's Sun Ra, perhaps the peak of the ensemble's favoring experimental improvisation rather than recognizable melodies (as with *Out in Space*, a minority element in the proceedings). And there is no doubt in the listener's ear that the Brits are more shocked than the French and the Germans by these extreme sonic assaults: applause begins to occur rather late into the first set (but one can hear the gradual learning curve towards the shock of the new).

The following year also proved to be a banner year for global touring, taking the Arkestra to such far-flung spots as Finland and Egypt. As in the case of Frank Zappa, Helsinki proved to be a highly accepting and inspirational venue. In 2009, Transparency issued a two CD and DVD coverage of Ra's performance there in October of 1971. Although these live versions tend to go on at some length (because there is a theatrical and dance element which the musicians are accompanying), this is a highly rewarding listen because of the sheer size and exuberance of the band. (And the recording quality is quite good.) "Love in Outer Space" gets a magisterial, highly percussive reading; "Watusi" provides polyrhythms galore when this large ensemble starts tub-thumping. The second disc features an extended, untitled flute interlude, some very soulful vocals on "Space Is the Place," bass minimalism on "Angels and Demons at Play" and a very funky "Second Stop is Jupiter" with wild shrieks from one of the female vocalists (I hope it's Wisteria el Moondew, then a member of the group!). They end this second set with some transcendentalist praise directed "To Nature's God" ("lightning, sunshine, wind, the leaves on the trees ... . Give some credit where credit is due") and an urgent invocation to "Prepare for the Journey to Outer Space" ("This world ain't gonna be here long ... . Time to go"). Fun stuff, and even a good set for initiating the novice listener: I got four people interested in Sun Ra's music by playing this material.

The accompanying DVD has a brief interview with Sun Ra where he mainly discusses the need for laws to provide alien visitors with some rights and protection, a reciprocal necessity in the space age (we'll need them when we visit other inhabited worlds). And while we're at it, how about some laws for angels too? Since Sun Ra believed he was an extraterrestrial and an angel, this might be special pleading. Fortunately, the Finnish interviewer takes it all in stride.

In 2010, Art Yard and Kindred Spirits jointly released *The Paris Tapes*, a concert at Le Theatre du Chatelet performed six weeks after the Helsinki show. Also extremely well-recorded, this set opens with a fine synthesizer workout, including ray-gun blasts of a highly percussive nature. "Discipline 27" really swings out and evolves into some trademark saxophone dueling among the usual suspects (Pat Patrick, Danny Davis, Marshall Allen, John Gilmore, Danny Thompson). A very sinuous rendering of "Somebody Else's Idea" (aka "Somebody Else's World") becomes a repetitive mantra with exotica lounge vocalese. As Knoel Scott says in the liner notes, "Watusi" showcases an "African Drum Choir," featuring James Jacson's Ancient Egyptian Infinity Lightning Wood Drum (carved from a tree struck by lightning in defiance of Native American taboos). The audience screams with delight at the intense results.

As with the Helsinki concert, "Space Is the Place" gets a very energetic reading (albeit quite different, more in the spirit of gospel shouting): "Your thought is free / And your life is worthwhile." "Angels and Demons at Play" (i.e., flutes and drums) also gets a different treatment than Helsinki. This concert concludes with a jaunty, rare unnumbered "Discipline" that evolves into an organ solo and a cacophonous horn and reed blowout followed by a synth solo with enough square wave action to break up a listener's kidney stone! Suitably big sounds from one of Ra's largest touring Arkestras ever (27 members including dancers and a light show coordinator).

The Arkestra finished up the year in Egypt, which resulted in three albums worth of live material from sundry concerts and television appearances. I think the best of these is *Horizon*, taken from a December 17 concert at the Ballon Theatre in Cairo (and sponsored by the Egyptian Ministry of Culture!). Noteworthy moments include the obscure "Discipline #2," a flute workout for Marshall Allen, Danny Thompson, and Danny Davis. The title track is another Ra synthesizer extravaganza. And "We'll Wait for You" (later known as "I'll Wait for You") is delivered as a poem, not a song by June Tyson (she includes the "like the lash of a whip" simile from the poem that would get deleted from the song lyrics; see below).

Stateside Live Appearances, Studio Work, and a Jaunt to Paris (1972-1975)

The recently released *Life Is Splendid* documents more thoroughly the Arkestra's 1972 performance at the Ann Arbor Blues and Jazz Festival (previously only briefly excerpted on a compilation album). This concert, the beginning of a three-year tradition for Ra, gave the band its best and biggest American reception to date. They more than rose to the occasion with wild "space ethnic" vocals, a fierce demonstration of African-inflected drumming on "Watusi," and the by-now trademark cosmo-spectacle.

A much rawer sounding but more thorough documentation of the summer 1972 Arkestra is available on Transparency's six CD box set *Live at Slug's Saloon*. Ra returned that summer sporadically to his former main venue during the New York residency. These tapes capture a June and an August show with slightly different personnel. The August show is by far the better of the two, although the June show captures a very gritty and grimy synthesizer solo (no one played the instrument like Sun Ra did—ever) and an organ solo that erupts into Vesuvian maximalism. (And for what it's worth, the long instrumental prelude of that show woke up a bat sleeping in my basement: Ra's effect on animals is always worth noting.)

The August date has an extended anti-apocalyptic gibe on "At First There Was Nothing": "Is that all you got to do? / Sitting around waiting for the end of the world? ... / You got to find something else to do." In any case, every Ra aficionado knows what the band later reveals: "It's after the end of the world. / Don't you know that yet?" The percussion workout on "Watusi" turns into a Haitian ra-ra procession replete with whistles. The new "Discipline 27-II" gets a lush, slightly different reading than the studio recording from around the same time (see below). But best of all, the August 19, 1972 version of "The Shadow World" gets into some really alien hybrid instrumentals cum vocalese, the true "space ethnic voices" promised on many a liner note.

These recordings confirm Los Angeles-based Transparency founder Michael Sheppard's claim that his label's partial specialty with regard to Ra is "the really psychedelic stuff from about 68 into 72, maybe even 73 or 74, where it's almost like they've stopped playing jazz entirely" (Gershon 111). In other words, Ra's avant-pop at its most avant—as much space liturgy as concert!

Around this same time the band made the studio recording *Space Is the Place* in Chicago. On first listen, I thought the title track was too repetitive; repeated listenings have opened up a lot of interesting elements in the piece: a fine horn chart, gentle Moog bleeps, gibbering ape noises in the back channels (it was originally released in quadraphonic four-speaker sound), a twisted overall funk effect that definitely shows Ra reaching out to a younger audience. In the original quad, or even in simulated surround sound, it offers a genuine soundscape. Ra was never interested in making concept albums, as noted. (After all, why make a conceptual album when your whole *oeuvre* is just one big concept / body of doctrine?) Nonetheless, his brief series of quad releases at least demonstrated that Sun Ra was beginning to take the vinyl record as a medium in its own right—one he could use in special ways to get his message across.

The other side of the recording provided a uniquely conscientious sampling of the Arkestra's variety: the classic inside jazz of "Images" with traditional piano and a lyrical tenor solo from Gilmore; "Discipline 33" 's Egyptian-sounding processional riff and space organ solo; "Sea of Sound" 's chaotic reed soloing; and finally, a reworking of the "Rocket Number Nine" space chant. Because of this range, *Space Is the Place* (not to be confused with the film soundtrack of the same name) might be a better place to start listening to Ra than any ostensible greatest hits collection.

During the same Chicago session date, the Arkestra also made the much more obscure Saturn release *Discipline 27-II*, a far more challenging affair but arguably an even more major work. "Pan Afro" demonstrates how close Gilmore could get to the feel of John Coltrane's tenor when he wanted to. "Neptune" is both a mellow sax jam and one of June Tyson's best space chants: "Have you heard the news from Neptune, Neptune, Neptune, Neptune?" The title track is Ra's major piece in the discipline series of compositions and his fullest musical sermon statement regarding his beliefs:

> For you, I gave everything I never had.
> They call this life?
> They really think this is life?
> This is not life.
> We know what life is.
> Life is splendid.

For the entire side of a record, we get these call-and-response doctrines repeated by Ra, June Tyson and the other ethnic space vocalists. The absurdity of terrestrial existence leads Ra to proclaim that "The world ended 3,000 years ago" and that we are "on the other side of time": "Where's your sense of humor? / Let's all have a good laugh." At which point the Arkestra cracks up, both vocally and with laughter replicated on the saxophones in emulation of the "laughing blues" novelty tradition. A remarkable record, and a thorough canvass of Ra's beliefs.

Around this time, because of the growing word-of-mouth reputation of the live shows and some critical recognition in jazz circles, Sun Ra was able to work with major labels as well as El Saturn. These mainstream flirtations happened throughout the later career in cycles, always ending in eventual abandonment by the major label in question. Despite his cult following, Ra has never been a way to wealth for the corporate music industry—not even by the more relaxed criteria for jazz music. *Space Is the Place,* for example, was released on Blue Thumb records (a pop label that took a few chances: e.g., Captain Beefheart's *Strictly Personal*).[6] But both artists only had one record on the label.

The big score of the early seventies, however, was an ambitious contract with ABC-Impulse. This was the most distinguished label for sixties jazz in America, after all, with an impeccable roster of artists that included John Coltrane, Pharoah Sanders, Archie Shepp, Albert Ayler, and McCoy Tyner (to name only a few). To be released on this label was in effect critical canonization as well as an economic proposition. ABC planned to reissue a massive 21 of the original Saturn records (an arrangement now actually realized by the smaller Evidence label) and contracted for four new releases (Szwed 333; Ed Michel, liner notes for *The Great Lost Sun Ra Albums*). This sweet deal soon went sour when the numbers came in.

Which brings us to the next Ra highlight, *The Great Lost Sun Ra Albums.* These were *Cymbals* and *Crystal Spheres,* two Impulse albums recorded in 1973 but never released until 2000. They are both superb instrumental albums. The highlight of *Cymbals* is "Thoughts Under a Dark Blue Light," a seventeen-minute "monumental soul blues" (Robert Campbell, liner notes). Replete with funky sax charts and generous helpings of Gilmore, Ra and Boykins, this track is an ultimate example of Ra's many engagements over the years with the blues form. (Highlights of Sun Ra's collected blues-based recordings would easily stretch to about 5 CDs.)

Crystal Spheres has a few equally ambitious moments. "The Embassy of the Living God" has a great deal of diverse soloing and reed ensemble work; "Sunrise in the Western Sky" contains THE major solo statement of tenor John Gilmore. This latter track is the only opportunity Ra ever gave him on record (or, as far as I know, in concert) to stretch out and blow as long as the major Coltrane solos. Needless to say, he could do it! His sax has a fabulously metallic sound, in part because of Ed Michel's professional production. Because of the depth of Ra's career-long collaboration with Gilmore and Marshall Allen, "Sunrise in the Western Sky" is an important document.

I would also like to mention a 1973 live recording, *Sun Ra live in Paris at the "Gibus"*—a club that attempted to emulate the vibe of the Arkestra's New York home base, Slug's, but was deemed "much too nice" for that comparison by the band (Szwed, *Space* 228). It's worth checking out for one standout track. "Salutations from the Universe" is a fifteen minute Moog and Space Master organ Ra solo that truly explores the absolute limits of the sounds these instruments can make. This music will clean out your ears, scare your pets and threaten your speakers. The rest is a good selection of what the large live ensemble was doing then (Ra originals, a Fletcher Henderson standard, etc.). The liner notes in the Italian reissue are hilariously (?) racist, dropping the n-bomb repeatedly ("Sun Ra was a n——") because of a mistranslation from the French *negre*. Someone needs to fix that.

Thanks to the 2009 reissue by Art Yard, one can also hear the 1974 El Saturn recording *The Antique Blacks* (off a live Philadelphia radio show on August 17 and unavailable for many years). This is an unusual set for several reasons. First off, it showcases a mellower and smaller Arkestra. The opening track, "Song No. 1" is mostly straight-ahead jazz, with a round of solos, spiced up by some alto wildness from Marshall Allen. The title is curious: is this Ra's first composition he considered a "song?" (Not that there are any lyrics.) This more relaxed sound anticipates later seventies releases such as *Lanquidity* and *Sleeping Beauty*.

Secondly, this outing features a lot of Ra's poetry, constituting a virtual tutorial for humans. The abundance of spoken word material (albeit mostly accompanied by the band) may reflect the absence of vocalist June Tyson—who in previous years held up the lion's share of the vocals. It may also reflect Ra's perceptions of the opportunities provided by a live radio broadcast to get his cosmic message out: an opportunity not to be squandered! And finally, this was the historical moment of Watergate and Nixon's resignation. Sun Ra could sense the confusion of the moment and use it to his advantage as a kind of messianic cosmic messenger. A few examples will serve as illustration (and bear in mind none of these pieces I'm quoting entered the standard Arkestra repertoire; they are relatively rare examples of Ra being totally in the historical moment, albeit in his own peculiar manner):

> They do not know how loud the silence can be ... .
> [They're on] the right road, the wrong direction ... .
> The arrow points to pointlessness ... .
> The people and the leaders walk hand in hand [on the right
>   road, wrong direction;
> they need to go to "space"] ("There is Change in the Air")

> The antique blacks belong to me ... .
> I plan to present them to the greater universe ... .
> I plan to place them in Lucifer's care [because Whitey fears Lucifer; *The Exorcist* is still in the mix!] ("The Antique Blacks")

> You would like to go into outer space, into our territory ... .
> We're all around you ... .
> We've been here a long time watching you ... .
> We are not your enemy

You refuse to be our friends ... .
Take the big gamble ... .
I am the magic lie greater than your truth ... .
You can't even take care of the fishes in the sea ... . [part of a larger environmental rap]
I will not let you go there [into space] until you learn how to treat me ... ,
[and yet, on the other hand]
Why don't you visit me?
You have nothing else to do.
And always remember:
If you are not my friends, I am not your enemy. ("You Thought You Could Build A World Without Us")

We have an intriguing set of shifting personae within these texts, a mixture of threatening and welcoming that perhaps ultimately derives from Michael Rennie's alien Klaatu in *The Day the Earth Stood Still*. As Ra repeatedly opined in text after text, humans are an immature species. The Man from Saturn can help them if they "treat" him right (which begins for any musician with money and perqs, of course!). In this context, "Song No. 1" is another carrot for the listener to balance the stick of Ra's semi-jeremiads. If not the first Ra you should hear, *The Antique Blacks* captures a very interesting and brief seized moment in a long, diverse career. And bottom line: the music's great. Gilmore is playing his most lyrical tenor saxophone and Sun Ra has utterly mastered the newer electronic keyboards with truly unearthly results.

Also of some transitional interest is the 2009 Leo release *Live in Cleveland* (January 30, 1975). The concert opens with a rare space chant called "Astro Nation": "We hereby declare ourselves to be of another order of being: / an Astro Nation of the United Worlds of Outer Space." Dale Williams funks the melody up with some fine electric bass. We also get an early version of the "I, Pharaoh" declamation (see below); in fact, one gets sonic whiplash by the transition from "I, Pharaoh" with its conjuration of ancient Egypt through an eight-minute synthesizer solo to an extended and lush reading of Duke Ellington's "Sophisticated Lady." This last homage—a classic big band arrangement especially highlighting the bass, Ra's piano and John Gilmore's tenor sax—serves as a harbinger of Ra's desire to integrate the Arkestra with jazz history as a whole in concert on a consistent basis (a tendency which began with the Fletcher Henderson covers at Slug's in the sixties but did not become standard Arkestra practice until the mid-seventies). Sun Ra wanted the Arkestra to do it all, pretty much—and they delivered! As does Ra himself, although his vocal delivery of the song ("smoking, drinking / never thinking of tomorrow") falls well shy of crooner status.

In 1974 and 1975, El Saturn records issued two of the rarest Arkestra recordings, the "*Sub Underground Series.*" These only became generally available in 2012, courtesy of England's Art Yard label. The 1974 album opened with "Cosmo Earth Fantasy," an extended free performance that actually dates back to the *Strange Strings* sessions in the late sixties. This piece is all about the lovely and unusual timbres; it is utterly unclassifiable, at the very limits of jazz (and not recognizable as such to most ears). There is no discernible melody line. The only jazz element is its improvisatory nature. After the opening strings, Sun Ra weighs in on Hohner Clavinet, eventually duetting with Marshall Allen on oboe. Ronnie Boykins plays some fuzzed-out bass, followed by wild and intense xylophone work from an unknown player which is eventually accompanied by Danny Davis on flute. This exploration hangs together as an esoteric listening experience—sub underground, indeed. There is a build-up to a sonic climax of xylophone, clavinet, bass, flutes and percussion. But one suspects, in a parallel to the structure of live Arkestra performances, Ra chose this side-long excursion as a way to scare off the casual listener. Sun Ra demanded unconditional acceptance from his listeners. They could have preferences and judgments, but he needed the right to play anything he was interested in. And he loved to stretch our ears: that's what "Cosmo Earth Fantasy" does, like the other *Strange Strings* work.

The second side of the original album rewarded the listener with three more accessible treats. First off, there were two numbers from a 1974 concert at Temple University. "Love is for Always" offers lyrical interplay between Ra on piano and John Gilmore on tenor sax. "The Song of Drums," with its African language singing against a drum line, could pass for African world music—but is in fact a Sun Ra composition. This paradox is also true for "The World of Africa," a 1968 rehearsal tape featuring June Tyson singing African vocals. Ra scholar Paul Griffiths lays this all out in the 2012 liner notes. When the album was first issued, the average fan assumed incorrectly it all came from 1974.

The 1975 Sub Underground release was even more peculiar, offering no track titles on the record. Side one of it was relatively tame stuff from 1962, two covers of jazz standards and two originals from other members of the Arkestra (a quite rare arrangement) that sounded like jazz standards. We have here an early rendition of "What's New" with great solos from Al Evans on flugelhorn and Calvin Newborn on electric guitar. Ra's approach to the song is typically unconventional, an upbeat reading lacking any of the lachrymose regret that most crooners bring to this material. "Wanderlust" and "Jukin' " follow (written respectively by Newborn and Evans). That side closes with a lovely and simple jazz quartet performance of "Autumn in New York" (Ra, Gilmore, Boykins on bass and Thomas Hunter on drums). Here is Ra at his most lyrical and accessible. Even my cats loved zoning out to this—always a sign of audio quality.

The second side is the joker in this particular deck, a space chant and declamation, eventually given the title "We Roam the Cosmos," from 1975. The fire and fury of this space sermon—as always, telling us to get off our mortal butts and "try something else than planet Earth"—anticipates some of the drama of the declarations made during the Detroit Jazz Center residency considered below. The combined series offered two sides of intense and uncompromising Ra bookending two other sides of the Arkestra in a mellower mood. The 2012 compact disk gives you all of it.

A weird side note: El Saturn kept reshuffling the material from the second release: one El Saturn release replaced "We Roam the Cosmos" with "The Invisible Shield"; another retitled it "What's New?" (it was originally just marked "Sub Underground Series") and substituted a Ra original ("State Street") and more standards for "We Roam the Cosmos." Odd behavior even for El Saturn.

Back in Europe (1976)

I have always been fond of *Live at Montreux* (1976); as with *Space Is the Place* (1972), this is a well-rounded introduction to the Arkestra's variety. It includes a reverential yet subversive cover of Billy Strayhorn's "Take the A Train." Thus, except for the absence of Ra's keyboards, *Live at Montreux* sounds like what you would hear if you could catch the touring Arkestra today.

The French studio recording *Cosmos* (on the Cobra label, also from 1976) offers several delights, including the lilting space chant "Moonship Journey." "Journey among the Stars" presents chamber jazz, with much flute exploration augmented by R. Anthony Bunn's electric bass and Ahmed Abdullah's trumpet. And "Jazz from an Unknown Planet" combines a fine Cadillac chart with a stirring round of solos from Abdullah, Ra and Gilmore.

The much harder to obtain *Unity* (the Italian Horo label, 1976) has a rare recording of "Halloween in Harlem," perhaps Ra's finest processional, featuring lots of electronic wizardry on the space organ and spooky horn charts. This song highlighted the Arkestra's Halloween shows, and was often accompanied with costumed dancers jumping into the audience. The album's title perhaps refers to his telescoping of past, present and future in the song selections (which are heavy on covers from Henderson and his peers).

The Late Seventies: Outburst of Productivity

The late seventies offered a proliferation of superb Ra releases. 1977 saw a live concert which eventually was issued as *A Quiet Place in the Universe*. This recording is another way to obtain "I, Pharaoh." Along with "Discipline 27-II," this is a major Ra sermon in which he reveals that he formerly "dwelt in Egypt land" in a "kingdom ... splendid without compare." He lost his kingdom, preserving only "the secret of immortality." Even as he urged his audience to travel the spaceways with him, Ra now asks us to become his servants: "Why don't you be my people now? ... Behold me—Pharaoh!" An interesting offer from the living myth which many accepted (and many more did not).

In that same year, Ra also issued two more recordings of solo piano (*Solo Piano Volume I* and *St. Louis Blues*; the first were two volumes on Saturn entitled *Monorails and Satellites*). As a player, Sun Ra splits the difference between the grand old stride stylings of Earl Hines and/or Jelly Roll Morton and the avant-garde sound clusters of Cecil Taylor, often in the same piece. The results are distinctive and memorable. *St. Louis Blues* extends the instrument experimentally in "Sky and Sun" (favoring the very upper end of the keyboard) and "I Am We Are I" (slamming and plucking the strings in the piano á la American classical composer [and John Cage mentor] Henry Cowell's "Banshee").

Somewhere over the Rainbow (Saturn, 1977) adds the Arkestra, but continues Ra's infatuation with the piano. In the title track, he takes you over the rainbow by creating a rumbling thunderstorm on the lower registers in juxtaposition with a gorgeous reading of the melody. Another version of "Take the A Train" has a lyrical piano introduction. "Make Another Mistake" chants more Ra philosophy:

> You made a mistake
> You did something wrong
> Make another mistake
> And do something right.

Words to live by which prompted one member of the Bloomington, Indiana, concert audience to yell "bellissimo" at song's end.

Some Blues but Not the Kind That's Blue (Saturn, 1977), except for the title track, consisted of cover versions of sundry jazz and popular standards. The introductions to all these pieces are unusual (especially so for the title track, which appears to be an edit from a completely different session). They offer oblique little Ra piano solos in their own right until he showcases the main melody. "My Favorite Things" is the expected nod to John Coltrane, with Gilmore producing some appropriate sheets of sound on the tenor.

The Morrison / Lawrence / Gross composition "Tenderly" opens with a quotation from Sun Ra's own piece "Interstellar Low Ways." It turns out the two pieces are very similar melodically in their opening phrasing.

The CD reissue on the Unheard Music series (2007) adds two earlier readings of "I'll Get By" with a different lineup. More interestingly, it adds an unreleased (and untitled) Ra original from the 1977 session. This piece offers some intense tenor soloing from John Gilmore which is even more rambunctious than that provided on "My Favorite Things."

The same year and label's *The Soul Vibrations of Man* is distinguished by an "Untitled Improvisation" with the wildest reed soloing in the recorded canon (in order, Pat Patrick or Danny Thompson, baritone; Marshall Allen, alto; John Gilmore, tenor). As noted above, there is plenty of this material available since it was a component of almost every Arkestra concert since the mid-sixties. But this is the most extreme example. I also recommend the Rhapsody Films video documentaries *Sun Ra: A Joyful Noise* and *Mystery, Mr. Ra* for video footage of what this activity looked like in performance. It was not only music, but also dance and theater!

This incredibly active and diverse year of 1977, lastly, also includes a live solo piano recital in Venice, available on Leo Records in CD format. It provides a great complement to the studio solo work and shows how readily Sun Ra all by himself with a piano could captivate a diverse audience. Offering a program which mixes improvisations, originals and covers of standards, Ra gradually heats up his reverential audience. "Love in Outer Space" soars as a lilting piano vehicle; his cover of "Take the A Train" ends in some piano-bashing that sounds like the train approaching the concert hall. His work on "St. Louis Blues" reminds us that Ra can deliver straight ragtime with the best of traditionalists. By the time he delivers a jaunty and lyrical reading of Jason / Burton / King's "Penthouse Serenade," Ra has the audience in the palm of his hand—giving him the confidence and authority to treat us to a rare solo vocal on a lovely version of "Angel Race." And he introduces the experimental improvisation which follows by telling the audience, "I want to invite you to attend the party in 1980 on Jupiter." Great stuff worth hunting for ... .

I have previously discussed the quasi-pop work of *Disco 3000* and *Lanquidity* (both from 1978), but I would add that the recent release on CD of the complete *Disco 3000* concert in Milan, Italy (January 23 1978) during Ra's extended Italian sojourn is well worth a listen. In addition to all the Crumar Mainman drum machine soloing by Ra, this quartet—Ra, Gilmore, Luqman Ali on drums and new member Michael Ray on trumpet and vocals (and a vocal assist from June Tyson)—burned long and hard. "Third Planet" features intense hard-bop interplay between Gilmore and Ali. The track called "Spontaneous Simplicity" (which may really be "Dance of the

Cosmo Aliens"; title labeling here is flawed) offers squiggly synthesizers juxtaposed with Ray's soaring funk trumpet. They introduce a live version of "When There Is No Sun," a lovely new song (off the Italian studio release *New Steps* on the Horo label). Gilmore, Ray and Ali harmonize on the typically vatic lyrics: "The sky is a sea of darkness / When there is no sun to light the way." After an explosive free jazz climax of simultaneous soloing at top volume, Ra calms everybody down with a completely straight piano rendering of "Over the Rainbow."

In 2009, an obscure Ra reissue label called "Atomic Records" released *New Steps*, one of two studio recordings done by this quartet for the Italian Horo label in early January 1978 prior to the Italian tour with its live recordings. The studio version of "When There Is No Sun"—the only vocal on the album—offers even more exquisite vocal harmonizing from Gilmore, Ali and Ray. The session also features a great run-through of the jazz standard "My Favorite Things" and some quirky Ra compositions, doubly rare in this quartet format, such as "Moon People" (Michael Ray creating goofy horn effects to simulate extraterrestrial chatter accompanied by Ra playing his Crumar Mainman like a cello), "Sun Steps" (a lyrical meditation on piano that builds to a Michael Ray solo and a wildly dissonant ending), "Friend and Friendship" (with good call and response between the piano and the horn and reed combo), "Rome at Twilight" (a sonic picture of the city's bustle that hearkens back to early Ra compositions like "Chicago USA") and "The Horo" (an extended workout for the entire quartet with much sensitive musical conversation).

Media Dream (1978) also features the quartet. The title track (almost) "Media Dreams" takes the listener on an interesting ride. Ra was fascinated at this point with the new keyboard synthesizers. He tinkers with quasi-minimalist "chords and obligatti," while Michael Ray soars around him (Szwed 349-50). The very rare recording *The Sound Mirror* from the same time has another major Ra sermon in its title track, as well as some mellow, "inside" Gilmore work ("Jazzisticology") and mostly solo sound sculpture for electronic keyboard ("Of Other Tomorrows Never Known").

By chronology of the original recording date, we next come to one of several Ra cosmic singularities, courtesy of the Transparency label: a 10 CD box set documenting three 1978 dates (with overall fine audio quality) of the Arkestra at Toronto's Horseshoe Tavern (with a bonus disk showcasing a 1968 Ra interview on Radio Pacifica). On the one hand, as Art Yard consultant Michael Anderson says disparagingly of the Transparency label, "Those are bootlegs ... . I don't know where those tapes came from." On the other hand, as Ra critic Pete Gershon notes, "even Ra's own releases of the Arkestra's music were often low budget affairs that were rather imprecise with respect to such details...[;] those aspects of the Transparency program might well have appealed to the intergalactic trickster" (Gershon 112). By all accounts, Transparency founder Michael Sheppard is in good standing with the surviving members of the Arkestra (which must mean among other things that he's helping them financially with his windfall).

I give this context because part of me says that if a slightly curious listener just obtained this one box set, they would pretty much have a thorough representation of what the mature Arkestra did as I described it at the beginning of my "Omniversal Listening Suggestions." From this one recording you could decide whether you wanted to delve deeper into Ra or whether you had heard "quite enough," as they say. To me as a Ra enthusiast, the most interesting show is the first one on March 13, 1978 (discs 1-3). This shows a Canadian audience responding to the band with more enthusiasm than I ever heard a European or American audience muster. At the final outer space altar call, for example, when Ra informs them "Get your tickets here please. Do you want one way or round trip?," they yell out "One way," "Take me with you," "Space is the place" while banging on beer mugs for percussion accompaniment and even chanting "day-o." (I said that they were enthusiastic, not sober.) Ra responds to their accolades by letting his hair down as much as I've ever heard Ra do in concert, going all the way back to *Spaceship Lullaby* days by interpolating "Stranger in Paradise" in "Discipline 27-II"—and even "As Time Goes By"! It's a sonic love feast unparalleled in the Ra discography.

All three shows feature interesting and radically different improvisations from the band before Sun Ra appears on stage. The March date showcases Michael Ray's trumpet in dialogue with the percussion section at some length; the September 27 preamble starts out with Egyptian snake charmer sounds evolving into trumpet, and a meditative exploration in the spirit of fusion-era Miles Davis without sounding derivative of it in any way; the November 4 show begins with electric guitar, drum and vibraphone interaction before an echo-laden trumpet enters at approximately 11:00, followed by reeds a minute later, bass and (at around 18:00) a trombone solo. Three completely different sets of textures and moods from almost the same personnel ... . Once Ra arrives, the three concerts are more similar but still satisfyingly varied. All three showcase a variety of jazz standards covered with great care and respect (e.g., Fletcher Henderson, Duke Ellington and the like), Ra sermons and compositions, and a wide variety of space chants.

There are a lot of little surprises and treats here as noted; the only major unprecedented weirdness is on disc 5 when one of the Arkestra declares himself to be the "Birdman" during "Love in Outer Space" (is it wild man Michael Ray?) and gives the audience a mix of instructions ("sing with the birds ... they are way out") and critiques of earthly mores ("all through history truthful men are shot"). The bonus disc reiterates many of Ra's ambiguities and mysteries to the interviewer. Ra admits his music is "slightly evil in a sense" (because it's beyond good and evil) and that he's a "world teacher," "a double order of being," conducting a "knower's ark" trying to remedy the sad fact that "black people in America have been deprived of beauty." There is abundant beauty—and strangeness—on these ten disks. As noted, for some this may be enough Sun Ra to satisfy them (or even an overdose?).

Ra ended the decade with a few more gems. *On The Other Side of the Sun* (1979), the New York program music of "Manhattan Cocktail" captured well the discord and complexity of the island and provided another instance when Ra's writing seemed curiously similar to that of Charles Ives (who also captured urban sounds in compositions such as "Over the Pavements" and "Ann Street").

The title track of *On Jupiter* (1979) is a lush seventies mellow jazz reading of a then-new Ra space chant destined to become a solid part of the later Arkestra repertoire ("On Jupiter, the skies are always blue"). June Tyson's lilting vocal is accompanied by suitable loping percussion and some very mellow piano from the man from Saturn.

"UFO" is the real ear-opener: Sun Ra doing straight-up disco! This is a serious commercial bid—far more so than the odd keyboards on *Disco 3000*. This is New York disco 1979: "UFO, UFO / Take me where I want to go." Lots of electric guitars, that signature beat white people can dance to ... it's all here. As with Neil Young's Shocking Pinks or Frank Zappa's doo-wop (or his disco for that matter), when you're a far-out avant-popist, the most radical move you can make is to go far in. There isn't a single second of free jazz or atonality on this track. It's as if Sun Ra noticed what George Clinton and P-funk were doing with his concepts with their Mothership Connection—not to mention Earth, Wind and Fire— and decided to school them by giving them back their own approach raised to a whole other level of teen appeal. This reading seems to be reinforced by the signifying nature of some of the lyrics intoned by Ra: "You can fool some of the people some of the time, / You can't fool all of the people all of the time."

"Seductive Fantasy" is the third and final track comprising *On Jupiter*. Here Ra works in his more typical proclivities. The composition begins by living up to its title with heavy wah-wah guitar and a fine piano accompaniment that evolves into a sinuous and rapid solo (all at once, a neat sonic trick which reminds us that Sun Ra has few musical limitations). A few raucous bursts from the horns and reeds break our trance and remind us that this is the Arkestra after all. Cello and violin interplay further unplug the fantasy until the piano returns to try to restore the mood, abetted by percussion and James Jacson on bassoon. Finally, a blast of the space key / chord and one last highly discordant piano note cluster ends this interesting and complex piece. What we hear here is a complex negotiation with a new audience, a willingness to meet them more than halfway as long as Sun Ra can reserve the right to take them out of the musical shallows into the cosmic depths (cf. Zappa's negotiations with the disco crowd on *Sheik Yerbouti*).

And then on *Sleeping Beauty* (also 1979) we find the mellowest Ra ever recorded, from his lush seasonal chant "Springtime Again" through "Door of the Cosmos" ("Love and life interested me so / That I dared to knock at the door of the cosmos") to the fractured fairy tale of the title track. Ra traffics in his own version of Zappa's conceptual continuity in the lyrics here. The juxtaposition of the tale of Sleeping Beauty with his desire "to speak of Black Beauty to you" at first glance seems to make little sense beyond ethnic inclusiveness (cf. Black Jesus or Black Barbie). And then, one recalls the 1968 Pacifica observation cited above where Sun Ra observes that "black people in America have been deprived of beauty." Eleven years later, Ra tries to rectify this state of affairs explicitly. Abetted by Damon Choice's vibraphone stylings and exotica-influenced background vocalizing, Ra directly addresses Black Womanhood: "I know you don't want to hear it ... . Without Prince Charming, there's nothing, Black Beauty ... . Nothing will ever happen." Ra insinuates that he is the Prince Charming in question that can wake Black Beauty by showing this Eternal Black Feminine her own beauty through his music. Such a claim and persona coming from this celibate, queer extraterrestrial transcends even his other outrageous masques as Satan or as Pharaoh. And yet his curiously gentle approach promises to seal the deal—and might have worked if a critical mass of African-American women had been listening! If you want Sun Ra in a very pleasant mood, this has been conveniently reissued on CD in the Unheard Music series.

Finally, *God Is More than Love Can Ever Be* (1979) presents Ra's music in a trio format (piano / drum / bass), which frees him up more for improvisation than on the solo piano recordings.

The 1980s

The first recording of the new decade worth mentioning for non-completist interested parties is a Transparency release called *Live in Rome* from March 28. The fine audio quality and abrupt breaks between songs eliminating applause (cf. Grateful Dead live releases) suggest that this double CD may have been originally intended for the Italian Horo label as a live album. Highlights include a flashy Michael Ray trumpet solo in the beginning of the concert that features his playing the impossible by holding a trumpet note for minutes with circular breath technique—and a comic closing gesture for the solo. We are also treated to a more piano-driven version of "Lights on a Satellite." As with the Swiss concert from a month previous issued as *Sunrise in Different Dimensions* (on Hat Hut / Art), there are a lot of older jazz standards covered; but in this show, Ra slips in his new "Springtime Again" amidst them (as a future standard?). There is even a rare new chant worth quoting in its wacky entirety, tentatively titled "Hit That Jive Jack":

> Hit that jive Jack
> Put it in your pocket till I get back
> I'm going to outer space as fast as I can
> I ain't got time to shake your hand

As Doctor John would say, mos' scosious!

Ra also released his first classical cover, a jazzy rendition of Rachmaninoff's "Prelude in C# Minor" (on the solo piano Saturn release *Aurora Borealis*). On *Dance of Innocent Passion* (also Saturn, 1980), Ra favored a theatrical organ sound on the title track (accompanied by light jazz guitar, drums and trumpet), "Cosmo Energy" (with arco bass and synthesizer), and "Omnisonicism" (with an appropriately wide range of timbres such as conga, saxophone, synthesizer and vibes). This latter adventurous set was recorded live at the Squat Theater in New York.

At the end of the year, the Arkestra recorded some even more challenging material excerpted from their 6-day, 11-performance residency at the Detroit Jazz Center. Two El Saturn releases emerged from this outing—and now there is a mammoth 28 CD Transparency release (2007). To consider the El Saturn excerpts first, *Beyond the Purple Star Zone* is worth checking out primarily for the deep space electronica of "Immortal Being." Also of some interest is the electric guitar soloing on "Romance on a Satellite" and the sweeping organ tone clusters on "Planetary Search" that suggest Sun Ra had been listening avidly to the Gyorgy Ligeti compositions in *2001: A Space Odyssey*, a decade earlier.

Oblique Parallax contained uncompromising Detroit moments as well such as "Vista Omniverse" for gritty, distorted organ and synthesizer, "Celestial Realms" for organ and Michael Ray's trumpet and "Journey Stars Beyond" for synthesizer (after a full-band free jazz introduction). After some of the cosmic hi-jinx on this last piece, an audience member (or an Arkestra member adding to the drama?) can be heard to marvel "What was that?" The Arkestra may have been aging and slightly mellowing, but they could still freak out their listeners if the stars were in proper alignment!

And then there's the 28 CD Transparency release of *The Complete Detroit Jazz Center Residency* by Sun Ra and the Omniverse Jet Set Arkestra (so named because he was into the newly discovered omniverse vs. the universe then [the former is even bigger!] and because the Jazz Center flew the band into Detroit?). Everything I said about the Horseshoe Tavern box set goes quintuple here: this is all the Sun Ra you might ever need—especially if you supplement it with downloads of "The Magic City," "Atlantis" and "Nuclear War." But it doesn't work that way, does it? A casual listener testing the waters with regard to an unfamiliar musical act doesn't begin with this much of a sonic investment! So, in actuality, this is an acquisition for hard-core devotees of the band. Since an exploration of this material as a result transcends the mere "Omniversal Listening Suggestions" promised early in this chapter, I have relegated my listening notes (with an ear towards absolute highlights) to an appendix.

Unsuprisingly, the Reagan presidency drew an aesthetic response from the man from Saturn. Sun Ra wrote the most political lyrics of his career in the early eighties in response to the nuclear buildup and the Strategic Defense Initiative. On the aptly titled *Ra to the Rescue*, he warned his audience on the otherwise lilting ballad "They Plan to Leave" of what was potentially in store:

> They plan to leave this world one day
> In sundry rocket ships to sail away
>
> They plan to go to somewhere there
> In splendid ships of models rare
>
> They plan to leave this world forever
> To lead the kingdom of Never-never
>
> They plan to find another place in the sky
> Without saying farewell, without saying goodbye
>
> They plan to put the White House on the moon, soon
> And the Kremlin on a satellite, soon

If the lyrics have an Oliver Stone paranoid tang, consider it a sign of those times. The High Frontier think tanks were probably not far off from Ra's accusations in their more speculative moments.

I have already mentioned Ra's best pop song, "Nuclear War." It is readily available on the reissued CD of the same name, but you will get more great music if you can find the two original Saturn Gemini releases: *A Fireside Chat with Lucifer* and *Celestial Love* (both 1982). On the former album (but not the *Nuclear War* CD) are "Makeup," a funky organ workout with lyrical Gilmore accompaniment, and "A Fireside Chat with Lucifer" itself. This latter piece takes up the entire second side of the album, deploying space organ, trumpet, theater organ, gentle electronics, piano, synthesizer and flute. What makes it unusual is its restrained, brooding and meditative quality—far from sixties and seventies extended rave-ups such as "Atlantis" or "Out in Space." The feel is closest to *Pangea*, the last music Miles Davis was recording in the seventies prior to a long sabbatical. Sun Ra seemed determined to explore at least once every jazz idiom that was ever attempted: here is his version of later fusion Miles.

On the original *Celestial Love* lp, one can find another version of "Interstellar Low Ways" (re-titled "Interstellarism" and re-orchestrated more for reeds and trumpet than flute) and a luscious cover of Duke Ellington's "Sophisticated Lady" (featuring Michael Ray on trumpet). The rest of the major material is on the much more easily accessible *Nuclear War*: "Retrospect," the appropriately dolorous ballad that follows both the title track on the CD and its appearance on *A Fireside Chat with Lucifer* (a rare example of Ra doing thematic sequencing!); "Blue Intensity," another funky organ vamp; and stellar covers of standards "Sometimes I'm Happy" and Charlie Chaplin's "Smile." This last has been redone by everyone from Nat King Cole to Michael Jackson. Sun Ra, June Tyson (on vocals) and John Gilmore offer the definitive reading here, even against this level of competition. Only on the CD version of these sessions do you also get "Drop Me Off in Harlem," another Ellington cover that switches from organ to full Arkestra.

In 1983, the following year, Sun Ra returned to Egypt and collaborated with drummer Salah Ragab, paying Ragab the rare compliment of recording two of his compositions with the Arkestra as well as letting him play on the recordings. "Egypt Strut" is a processional march (Ragab directed military bands). Eloe Omoe plays marvelous bass clarinet here, and the tune has a fine hook of an Egyptian cast. Also on the compilation *The Sun Ra Arkestra Meets Salah Ragab in Egypt* is "Dawn," with a melody based on an Islamic hymn suitable for that time of day. Ra delivers the melody on a Hohner Melodica; the Arkestra churns up a mean percussion line; Gilmore delivers another splendid tenor solo. (The Egyptian jazz from Ragab's band fills out the record nicely; the CD version has additional jazz from Ragab in a "free" vein as well as another Arkestra track, an epic live version of "Watusa" [aka "Watusi"].)

Stars That Shine Darkly (Volumes 1 and 2) contain two sides (one on each lp) of the 1983 Montreux festival concert by the Sun Ra All Stars. Besides Ra, Gilmore and Allen, this band featured jazz masters Archie Shepp and Don Cherry (who was later destined to make several more recordings with the Arkestra) as well as members of the Art Ensemble of Chicago, Lester Bowie and Don Moye (Szwed 356). It was a veritable supergroup of avant-garde players, and the results do not disappoint. The title of their collective improvisation (also "Stars That Shine Darkly") refers to black holes: like the astrophysical phenomenon, this band also combines blackness with great power and force. Archie Shepp's saxophone solos deliver gorgeous full tones; Richard Davis supplies memorable bass; John Gilmore offers another workout; Ra contributes a thunderous piano solo; Lester Bowie adds some characteristic comic effects on trumpet. This nonce band sounds like they've been conversing all their lives. (Or at least keeping tabs on each other's efforts!)[7]

The second side of the first volume is devoted to "Hiroshima," another composition evincing Sun Ra's nuclear concerns. The atomic bombing of Hiroshima, like the Holocaust or the events of September 11th, is a challenging subject for program music. Arguably, it can't be done. But then again, Ra was always interested in the impossible. The meager body of music about Hiroshima falls into two general categories: soft requiem pieces (such as Hikari Oe's subtle yet moving "Hiroshima Requiem") or attempts to convey the horror of the devastation through sound (Krystof Penderecki's "Threnody for the Victims of Hiroshima"). This piece by Ra is solidly in the latter tradition ("Retrospect" on *Nuclear War* might be an example of the former approach). "Hiroshima" is a giant theatrical organ solo accompanied by drums and percussion. The music combines ominous low notes with Japanese-inflected melodies. Its feel is gothic, intense and pained. Although Penderecki's composition remains the best ever written on this somber theme, Ra's work manages to convey his sincerity and concern. How amazing that it took Ronald Reagan to overtly politicize Ra's music, a body of work which largely avoided terrestrial politics throughout the sixties.[8]

By this time, given the Arkestra's arduous touring schedule, live recordings came to dominate the recorded canon. To make this generalization concrete (using Robert Campbell's discography in Szwed), between the 1983 studio session in Egypt with Salah Ragab and Ra's earthly demise, the Arkestra issued four times as many live recordings as studio releases. Once again I would state that all of this is good, but a few of the live recordings deserve special mention. A case in point would be *Love in Outer Space*, a December 1983 concert from Utrecht. Although there are no rarities on it, this disk offers a classic eighties Arkestra set with the band in fine mettle: its virtue is its well-delivered typicality of this nevertheless atypical music.

This version of "Fate in a Pleasant Mood" has a definitively lyrical piano introduction and fabulous hand drumming at its conclusion. The Utrecht audience were also treated to a stately cover of " 'Round Midnight" (with memorable solos from Gilmore and Ra) and a well-drummed version of the title track with superior piano accompaniment.

The 1984 *Live at Praxis* concerts from Athens, Greece reveal the Arkestra in a longer performance format (3 albums). The interesting material here includes a version of "Nuclear War" with alternate lyrics ("First comes the heat / And then comes the BLAST!"), Marshall Allen soloing on the *kora* (an ancient African string instrument made from a gourd and used by *griots*), a rare cover of "Mack the Knife" replete with vocal tribute to Louis Armstrong, another rare cover of "Satin Doll" and an early version of the Egyptian-inflected processional march "Carefree." The Arkestra always rose to the occasion when they visited locations associated with antiquity; NASA missed a good bet by not inviting them to play the Kennedy Space Center! (After all, outer space was always the matching bookend for the ancient world in Ra's cosmology.)

A Night in East Berlin (1986) features a lovely piano reading of "Interstellar Low Ways" and a wild battle royal on "The Shadow World" that whips even subdued East Berliners into a Dionysian frenzy. The CD version contains an amazing bonus track ("My Brothers the Wind and Sun #9" from the otherwise impossibly hard-to-obtain last Saturn vinyl release *Hidden Fire 2*). This extended piece of improvisatory chamber jazz from space most closely resembles "Stars That Shine Darkly"—although it is much more exotic. Since it was recorded live at New York's Knitting Factory, the Arkestra picked up a few extra alumni who prefer not to tour. Most notably, Art Jenkins returns for extraterrestrial scat with his space ethnic voice filtered through various horns. Combined with lots of violin and synthesizer textures, this music may be as close as Ra ever came to making really alien jazz with equal emphasis on both terms. I pity the poor fool who showed up for this gig on any hallucinogen; the Arkestra was playing the Bellevue waltz that night! Would that the rest of this music be released; it's truly one of the Arkestra's last post-avant-garde hurrahs.

I have already alluded to Ra's late-career fascination with the music of Walt Disney. The 1988 anthology *Stay Awake* has only one track from the Arkestra, "Pink Elephants on Parade." But that cut is so fabulously carnivalesque that it's worth obtaining for that reason alone—and there are other delights to be had as well on the disc, ranging from Yma Sumac to Ringo Starr with Herb Alpert. If you want much more of the same, *Second Star to the Right (Salute to Walt Disney)* is indispensible, even though it's a CD derived from an audience tape. This 1989 concert from at the Jazzatelier in Ulrichsberg, Austria, displays the band in high surrealist mode as they romp through a series of Disney film tunes. "The Forest of No Return" proves a perfect marriage between the mouse and Ra—the only Disney lyric with the earthbound claustrophobia and paranoia Ra felt about this planet ("You can scream, you can shout / But you can't get out"). "Zip-A-Dee-Doo-Dah" transforms the song's original minstrelsy into a vague menace behind the grins, more than hinted at by Marshall Allen's squiggly alto solo. The highlight of the session is the title track, surely one of Disney's most haunting songs, here rendered reverentially by Ra through piano and vocal. "Heigh Ho! Heigh Ho!" and "Whistle While You Work" seem to be caught between being paeans to discipline and quasi-Marxist critiques of the exploitation of the workers. This tension, I think, results from the gap between what Ra intended the songs to convey and the subtexts delivered by the Arkestra's performance of them. (Easier to hear than explain.) From either perspective, the point is that these last two covers will last longer than you want to hear them. And be it discipline or exploitation, from either perspective that is precisely the point. After listening to this music, you will never think of Disney the same way again.

Final Recordings, or, Sun Ra Leaves Earth

All of Ra's later studio releases have something to recommend about them (for example, *Blue Delight* [1988] has an exquisite version of "Days of Wine and Roses"). But the best of these is *Mayan Temples* (1990), his last studio recording with the Arkestra. Ra reworks older material such as "El Is a Sound of Joy" and "Theme of the Stargazers" into updated, extended and more lush versions. One key difference in these readings is his addition of rich synthesizer textures to the original piano melodies. And "Sunset on the Nile" is the last great Ra composition, a mood-setter with sumptuous polyrhythms that transcends even such idylls as "Springtime Again." This final track ends Ra's studio career with his band on a grand note of sublime closure.

The late live recordings kept coming, though. There are moving rarities such as June Tyson's violin solo, as fragile as a spider's web, on "Discipline 27" (*Stardust From Tomorrow*, 1989 concert). There is even exuberance, as Michael Ray plays the jester to get us to give up a smile. But there is also the sadness of encroaching mortality, most evident in the way "We Travel the Spaceways" comes to sound like a dirge on these late recordings. It had been a long road, and the travelers were weary.

Despite the exuberance of an opening romp through "Frisco Fog" and a fun "Blue Delight" (with Michael Ray quoting from Gershwin's "Rhapsody in Blue" for a few bars), the dominant note of the *Live in London 1990* concert is struck by a somber cover of Lalo Schifrin's "Down Here on the

Ground." Ra's vocal laments his earthbound, mortal status: "Down here on the ground / Is not a place for living." He finds himself "wanting something better ... wanting something more"—to emulate the birds "flying so free ... . If you hear this sound / Down here in the ground / It's only me trying to fly." Sun Ra delivers this vocal with a haunting stoicism that the concluding space chants' promises of interplanetary travel cannot mollify.

And further ironies abound when the first post-stroke live recording (*Friendly Galaxy* from Montreuil, France, in 1991) ends with the band announcing that t-shirts are for sale after the concert. Like Gustav Mahler before him (who scored his fatal heart arythmia into his ninth symphony), Ra knew how to put his own dying into his music both thematically and sonically. These concerts are important documents, but definitely not preferred entry points into Ra's music. The aftertaste of soul fatigue is too much to offer the novice listener; it can be appreciated and respected only after some exposure to Sun Ra and the Arkestra at their peaks.

Sun Ra ended his career in a strange double register. On the one hand, *Destination Unknown* (1992) is a joyous last live recording from the Moonwalker Club in Aarburg, Switzerland. The melancholy of later live works such as *Stardust from Tomorrow* and *Friendly Galaxy* is missing as the band cooks through a pleasing mix of standards and Ra compositions and chants. If one didn't know better, that is. For by this time singer, dancer and violinist June Tyson was unable to tour, fighting the breast cancer that would end her life that November; Gilmore was also absent, declining from emphysema (Szwed 376). This band sounds reinvigorated because the elder statesman in it is the healthy Marshall Allen (the now-marginalized Ra recovering from his strokes). Trumpeter Michael Ray is really directing this show, a trial run for his own post-Arkestra ensemble (Michael Ray and the Cosmic Krewe). He even gently tweaks the master during a now-joyous "We Travel the Spaceways," asking him if he's fastened his seatbelt and assuring the audience "Ra's all hooked up"—a somewhat grim joke given Ra's wheelchair-bound status. At the set's conclusion, he exhorts the small audience to "Give it up for Sun Ra." It's a fun time, but it's more Michael Ray's joy than Ra's at this point.

On the other hand, Ra's last studio recording, *A Tribute to Stuff Smith* (1992), offers more satisfying if melancholy closure. This is really violinist and former Arkestra member Billy Bang's record. Bang leads a quartet including Ra on keyboards, Thelonious Monk and Arkestra alumnus John Ore on bass and Cecil Taylor alumnus Andrew Cyrille on drums. Ra had turned his disability to advantage by offering wild melodic leaps of faith in his perforce simplified solos. As Steve Holtje says in the liner notes about Ra's solo on "Only Time Will Tell": "Almost any pianist could play it—but only Ra would think of it." The eight-song set covers standards associated with violinist Stuff Smith, including a haunting version of "Lover Man." But the epiphany is "Deep Purple," a song Ra played with Stuff Smith on Ra's very first recording. If one has any doubts of Ra's sense of his imminent departure from Planet Earth, consider the significance of his re-recording the first song he ever taped on this, the last session he ever played on in his life. If you're enthralled by now with Ra's previous work, you'll want to take this sentimental journey with him.

Let me emphasize that this has been an extremely truncated overview—believe it or not!—of some of the highlights of Ra's music (in my humble opinion). I have discussed less than half of his recorded output, and would not dissuade the committed or even interested party from any of it. Sun Ra had too much integrity to put out half-baked playing, even if the technical standards of many of these sonic documents are palpably lower than industry standards. Which begs the question: would you prefer the well-recorded treacle of Wynton Marsalis or Kenny G., or the sometimes rough-cut diamonds (stardust from tomorrow) of the Arkestra? We know where Ken Burns stands. But as Ra would ask, what's your story?

Posthumous Discoveries and Tributes

Discoveries

As I have been indicating in this march through the catalogue, a great deal of material has been released since Sun Ra's departure from Earth in 1993. In addition to John Sinclair's release of tapes from the Ann Arbor Blues and Jazz Festival, no less than five labels have emerged that are heavily invested in making Ra's music available to the listening public: Leo Records, Evidence Records, John Corbett's Unheard Music series, Transparency and Art Yard. Transparency and Corbett have also been releasing DVDs of films featuring Sun Ra and / or Arkestra performances. The result is that a search on Amazon, for example, will turn up nearly 400 Sun Ra recordings and a double-digit amount of video material. This readily makes him the most prolific musician I am considering in this book.

In fact, so much is out there that it's easier to say what's not available. As alluded to above, the complete *Hidden Fire* recordings (as opposed to the teaser excerpt on *A Night in East Berlin*) are the only major Ra music a fan might want to hear that is not readily available (as of fall 2013). Everything else is well-documented. I have discussed some album reissues and new concerts made available above in the chronological order of their original performance. Let me devote a little time here to some numbered series of releases— Transparency's 6 live DVDs, the "Audio Series," and their later "Lost Reels" audio series—as well as to a consideration of some of the more important tribute recordings, including the Arkestra's continuation after Sun Ra as a "ghost band" under the direction of Marshall Allen.

Transparency's DVD series is a motley assortment of performance footage ranging from professional editing with multiple cameras to a single camera held by an audience member. The tradeoff is a chance for new fans to see Ra in performance at the expense of optimal visuals. The first volume of these releases, *Sun Ra Arkestra Live at the Palomino* (November 5, 1988; North Hollywood) offers a case in point.

On the one hand, the footage is somewhat low-fi: an audience member who knew how to work a zoom on his (I presume the gender) video camera. Nonetheless, the concert has some real surprises. Because of that early November date, we get a super-rare performance of "Halloween in Harlem" in all of its splendor: monster movie chord changes, Frankenstein lurches from the dancers, spooky cackles and calls of "trick or treat." As the title of the piece indicates, Ra uses this composition to super-size the racially exotic. Since the 1920s, white bohemians have wanted to check out Harlem. Here's Halloween in Harlem, the Other raised to the nth power: the African-American as the monstrous in this problematic culture. (And maybe a sly concession that Ra knows he's in costume?) Michael Jackson was making similar connections in "Thriller," but Ra gets the slam dunk here!

This performance also has plenty of footage of Michael Ray playing the (wise) fool, flirting bodaciously (and archly) with the women in the group on a cover of "Easy to Love" ("It gets no better than this")—and playing a mean trumpet. Despite its technical deficiencies, this DVD will get the casual viewer interested in What The Heck Is This Guy Up To: the primal scene of a Ra encounter.

The second volume is another mixed bag. There are two sets from a 1986 show in East Berlin which are professionally shot in black and white (with faded picture quality). The visuals allow us to see the big band choreography (no dancers or women on this outing). And there are some musical highlights: a shimmering and ethereal synthesizer solo on "Prelude to a Kiss," a stately and deliberative reading of "Interstellar Low Ways," a bopping Gilmore solo on "Velvet." The show-stopper, however, is the "Shadow World" encore. The band shakes up the polite audience by tearing up the stage: throwing chairs around, twirling on the floor while playing their instruments, even going up to cameramen and making insane grimaces into the lens. The audience goes wild, of course, at this serious extraterrestrial invasion of the eastern bloc—a somewhat wilder affair than, say, a Billy Joel concert in Moscow!

Also on this DVD is a filmed segment of one of the Sun Ra All Stars shows from 1983 (for symmetry from West Berlin). This footage is of very high quality: color, multiple cameras on stage, professionally shot. I have discussed the music from these shows above; what the visuals add is a sense of Ra's bizarre leadership of this avant-garde ensemble. He'll do some hand conducting with little symbolic gestures that the band obligingly responds to in some mysterious fashion. Then he'll sort of prowl around the stage, hovering near individual players to listen to what they're trying to do. After that, he'll head back to his keyboards and throw a musical idea out. In contrast to the absolute power Ra wielded over his Arkestra, this looks more like herding cats. (And Lester Bowie, Don Cherry, Archie Shepp, Famoudou Don Moye and Philly Joe Jones are some mighty hep cats indeed!)

The third DVD has three separate concerts. The first is off Italian television, excerpting a solo piano concert by Sun Ra from Venice in 1978. There is some documentary footage of him walking along the canals and telling the interviewer that one's "ears have to be in tune with the cosmos" to appreciate his music. The actual concert footage shows Sun Ra in subdued costume (black and white colors and a beret) playing three original compositions for piano. His general approach, as always with his own solo piano pieces, is to alternate between thunderous dynamics and dramatic blurry fast runs (Conlon Nancarrow compositions played live instead of punched into a piano roll) and heartbreakingly gentle lyric explorations: the paradoxes of the omniverse.

The second concert is the visual record of the July 9, 1976 Arkestra concert at the Montreux Jazz Festival (released as the double album discussed above). As one will see, the visuals were half the show. He had a bevy of talented and energetic dancers in leotard, with outer-space accent, accompanying the space tunes (vs. the standards, which highlight the big band). Close-up camera work allows one to observe the hyperkineticism of Marshall Allen in alto sax skronk mode (a much better view than one ever got at an actual live show). Sun Ra flails on the electronic keyboards—at one point he's playing them behind his back. And what you SEE in the piano intro to "Take the A Train" is a man possessed by the spirit of music in Dionysian abandon. (You can only hear a little of that on the audio recording.)

The third show is from an outdoor public plaza in Lugano, Italy from 1990. Despite the late date, the Arkestra is as energetic as they were in the earlier glory days. Sun Ra hand-conducts them in a similar manner to Frank Zappa before "Discipline 27-II" cuts in. We see the band marching around on stage (on "I'll Wait for You"), more close-up Allen skronk (on the deconstructed "Prelude to a Kiss") and another crazy sax duel on "The Shadow World" (as in the second volume, but here in color). Younger electric bass and electric guitar players give the music a slight jazz-rock accent. The footage ends with a rare live recording of the late composition

"Sunset on the Nile" (from *Mayan Temples* in 1990, his elegy to all things Egyptian—and life itself). In addition to the beauty of the tune, we get an electronic keyboard solo and some appropriately thematic dancers.

The fourth DVD volume is a 1987 performance at the Pacifica Radio Cap City Jazz Festival in Washington, D.C. (the same FM station whose playing of back-to-back Sun Ra in 1993 told me that he must have died). The source of this material is a semi-professional audience tape (one camera, but good zooms and close-ups). I will only consider here the unusual aspects of what is a good, but fairly typical Arkestra outing (insofar as one can ever apply the word "typical" to this group). The highlights all come well into the concert. First off, we have a highly satisfying visualization of "Love in Outer Space" with a choreographed swaying horn section. The dancers somersault, tumble and give pelvic thrusts. John Gilmore works the drums instead of his saxophone. June Tyson not only dances, but provides the only occasionally heard vocal for the song: "sunrise in outer space / love for every face."

Then Sun Ra steps up to the microphone for a relevant thematic cover of "I Dream Too Much: "I only dream to touch your heart ... . / My dreams have shown / Perhaps I dream too much alone." A big percussion break (including moving drummers for a carnival atmosphere) segues into "I'll Wait for You" and a generous sampling of space chants (I count ten distinct ones). The show-stopper here is the final one, "Greetings from the Twenty-first Century which Ra hand-tailors for the Washington audience to their obvious delight:

> There's no need to cry. I'm with you now ... . I'm here now, I'm watching nations. They must do right. I am an agent of the living God. I'm watching every world including the USA. If they worship God, they must not kill. Because every person is a child of God.

As he declaims, the band exits but returns for an encore of "Spaceship Earth," a reminder to the audience that they need to pay their union dues for the "Fellowship of the Brothers of the Universe" and a final blast of the space key.

This DVD also has bonus footage of the Rufus Harley Quintet at the same festival apparently on the theory that Sun Ra fans will like this guy too. Harley plays more conventional jazz, but he packs a serious joker in his deck: he plays jazz bagpipe (in a kilt, no less)! You have to hear and see his bagpipe versions of John Coltrane's "A Love Supreme," "Greensleeves," "Stormy Weather" and "Amazing Grace" to believe them—not to mention his jazzy versions of various Scottish bagpipe melodies.

Volume Five has two New York area concerts from 1989: most of a set from the Lone Star Roadhouse in the Big Apple itself and a generous chunk of a performance at the African Street Festival in Brooklyn. The two dates must be fairly close together: the band personnel are the same (including a guy who does call-and-response bird noises with the audience during the warm-up) and both shows have a rare, zany cover of "Let's Go Fly a Kite" from *Mary Poppins*. The Lone Star gig is very heavy on the Walt Disney, in fact: we also get "Wishing Well" and "Zip-A-Dee-Doo-Dah" (this latter always a mind-bending performance of ironic minstrelsy). There also seems to be an exotic instrumental arrangement of "When You Wish Upon a Star" that only flirts with the melody.

The Brooklyn concert begins by having a giant puppet with a man inside (in the Caribbean these are called "Mocko Jumbies") lead Sun Ra onstage while embracing him—a theatrical gesture Ra imitates later by hugging and moving with a young female dancer in the Arkestra. He varies the opening space chants to tell the audience "this world is not your home" (either). Michael Ray contributes an arch vocal on "East of the Sun." Besides another soaring rendition of "Let's Go Fly a Kite," the other rarity here is a vocal performance of "Africa" (highly appropriate given the occasion). Unfortunately, the tape runs out before the piece ends.

The last DVD in the series (to date) is certainly the latest video footage of the Arkestra with Sun Ra I've ever seen (although I personally saw a show from a later date). It's two complete sets from Oakland, California on November 2, 1991. The sound is mono; the camera work is semi-professional (smooth zooms, good close-ups [you have to love James Jacson working that infinity drum]). The position is from stage right. The advantage of this set-up is an unusually intimate glimpse of the band; you can actually hear titles being called out on occasion. The downside is that Sun Ra's keyboards are on stage left, so all you see of him is an occasional head sticking above the instruments. But his health is already in decline. He's in a wheelchair (as when I last saw him) and he does not interact with the audience at all aside from playing and singing a few muted vocals in chorus.

The other Arkestra members pick up the slack and give the audience the sonic spectacle they came for (with special kudos to baritone saxophonist Pat Patrick, John Gilmore, Michael Ray and Marshall Allen). There is a dancer as well. On the one hand, this is an unusually conventional concert for this group: they take turns soloing like a regular jazz ensemble, stretching out each number in a way Ra would not consistently do in his prime. But the good news is that this show spotlights many wonderful pieces in the playbook that would only sporadically be played in concert ("Interstellar Low Ways," "Planet Earth," "El is the Sound of Joy"). "Opus in Springtime" is a mellow rarity from *Mayan Temples* (1990) with several bracing tenor solos from John Gilmore.

Perhaps the most telling moment in the concert is at the end of the second set. The concert closer is not a medley of space chants (there are none in the show; at the end of the first set "We Travel the Spaceways" is performed as a song not a chant) or a rousing "Space Is the Place" (not done at all in the show). Instead we get "They Plan to Leave." In its original context of the Reagan era, it was a jeremiad about world leaders planning to leave Earth to be safe from seemingly imminent nuclear war. As performed here, it's a haunting and melancholy song of departure. "They" are the Arkestra, and especially Sun Ra. As the song continues, the band leaves the stage, one by one; Sun Ra is escorted off; only Marshall Allen and another member abide to get the audience to give it up for Ra—and sell some merchandise. No admirer of this music will be unmoved, As T. S. Eliot says in "The Hollow Men," "This is the way the world ends / Not with a bang but a whimper."

To turn to their audio offerings, the first Sun Ra set of CD releases for the Transparency label, before individual projects and the "Lost Reels" series, were several concerts simply labeled the "Audio Series." Volume One, a somewhat inauspicious start, was recorded at Myron's Ballroom in Los Angeles (4/2/81—just a few months after the Detroit residency). It's not that it's a bad Arkestra performance; in fact, it's a rather generous one at over three hours. The audience is enthusiastic; the band is delivering on all booster rockets. The problem is that it is for the most part a very standard Arkestra show in its offerings as opposed to the idiosyncrasies that merit a live recording. Nothing unusual happens until the second disk, which features a rather carnivalesque reading of "Enlightenment." The band turns the lyric "strange mathematics, rhythmic equations" into a background chant for the other lyrics and a few Ra declamations. Not too unusual, but noteworthy when everything else so far was by the book (albeit Sun Ra's book).

The third disk gives us Sun Ra's creation myth in a brief sermon: "At first there was nothing ... . Nothing turned itself inside out and became something." (As good as any I've heard or read.) We also get a solid reading of "Lights on a Satellite" with shimmering piano and a gorgeous, restrained John Gilmore tenor solo. "Springtime Again" is equally lilting, courtesy of June Tyson's vocals and Gilmore (again)—the right song for a gig in early April. And finally, Ra's prophecies over the concluding "Discipline 27- II" optimistically predict "Someday soon there'll be shuttles to the moon." At least in *2001: A Space Odyssey* ... .

The Audio Series Volume Two release—a live date from December 14, 1985, at Club Lingerie in Hollywood—is far more indispensable for both the completist and the curious investigator of the spaceways. I suspect this show was inspired by the decadent location (even the name of the venue speaks volumes). In any case, we get a concert that Nathaniel West would have enjoyed. You won't even mind that it's an audience member's tape (the loud clapping close to the microphone gives it away now and then); the audio quality is quite adequate.

June Tyson does a variation on the "Mystery" invocation of Sun Ra: he is "the king of the kingdom of Mystery." Ra also deviates from the standard script by saying he has "names of splendor" and "names of shame," choosing to focus on the latter: "I am Sin!" Ra proceeds to explore his somewhat cheesy dark side (and ours):

> When they close the door
> And the lights are low
> What do they do?
> They s-i-i-i-i-i-nnnn! [with Ra's version of melisma!]

He brings "pleasure without measure" to "five million people" (a kind of Doctor Evil low-balling number!). Amidst this hilarious rap the band interrupts for a funky low-down-and-dirty jam. Can you be funky and funny at the same time? If you're the Arkestra, you can.

The "sin" rap is a tacit criticism of the Hollywood audience, however good-humored, which is continued in the "Discipline 27-II" sermon: "If I told you I was from outer space, you wouldn't believe a word I said. Would you? Why should you? ... You lost your way; you should have nothing to say ... . You can't go to Saturn. You can't go any place ... . Shame." After this chastisement of sorts, he kisses and makes up with a fine cover of "Prelude to a Kiss" replete with jazz guitar grace notes and witty alto skronk from Marshall Allen.

The typical mix of standards and Sun Ra compositions follow, but even here there's a nice curve ball: a rare cover of "Mack the Knife" which features a band member doing a cod impression of the Louis Armstrong vocal (that wacky Michael Ray?) and an extended tenor solo of the highest lyricism from John Gilmore. After Ra takes over the vocals, he even lets Gilmore end the song by himself with an extended and witty solo (it ends with the "shave and a haircut, two bits" riff).

The highlights of the second disk include a bravura Ra solo piano composition which segues into and interweaves with "Over the Rainbow": he enjoys alternating between the two texts. Obviously, it's an appropriate cover for film land. Even the concluding space chants / ring shouts have a little something extra in the mix in the form of an additional and rare chant: "No news is good news on Planet Earth." Announcer Brendan Mullen describes Sun Ra at show's end as "the Emperor of the Omniverse" in tribute to his regal performance.

Transparency also issued a nonce project on CD, *Untitled Recordings*, which doesn't fit into any of their other categories of the Audio Series, specific residencies or tours, or the Lost Reel series. Although it may not be for all casual listeners, it is curious enough to be worth mentioning—especially if one wants a look behind the scenes. The release has three separate components. The first is an audience tape from a 1985 Brooklyn concert with a quintet featuring Sun Ra, John Gilmore, Art Ensemble of Chicago percussionist Don Moye and New York Black Arts Movement jazz fixtures Andrew Cyrille on drums and Milford Graves on bass. The highlight here is "Opus in Springtime," which gets pretty free between Gilmore's tenor skronk and Sun Ra's frantic organ work.

The real rarity is the second text, a tape of a Sun Ra rehearsal at the band's Philadelphia house from circa late 1978. As with some of the recently released Frank Zappa rehearsal tapes, you get to hear the training process: Sun Ra doing a vocal scat of the desired performance, calling out the chord changes and indicating where performers should take solos. All this may be too technical for some, but it will certainly interest those with any musical background and dispel any notions that the Arkestra were playing it fast and loose on stage. Sun Ra was a diligent taskmaster. The best thing here—everything else involves rehearsing standards—is a Ra composition called by him "Tone Poem #9." This exquisite piece was scored for the reeds and horns (John Gilmore and Michael Ray eventually take solos). Given the melody and the date involved, I suspect the piece evolved into "Springtime Again" off *Sleeping Beauty*.

The other treat from the rehearsal tape is the weird dialogue among the band members as the session winds down. Sun Ra in a matter of fact way talks about encountering people who have risen from the grave (they smell like "mildew") and a musician who said that he "died in Casablanca." Another member of the Arkestra (Gilmore?) brings up the guy they saw at a concert with actual green skin. Oddly enough, this is exactly what one might think this band would be talking about! Such uncanny interests were all part of the esoteric package of Arkestra membership and communal living.

The final part of the CD is an at-home jam session from 1973 showcasing bass, synthesizer, reeds and trumpet. Good stuff, but not as revelatory as the rehearsal.

Transparency's final series, *The Lost Reel Collection Volume One: The Creator of the Universe* offers some real rarities. The first disk is from a June 1971 concert at the Warehouse in San Francisco. After a "Discipline" piece of unknown number, there are twenty minutes of Sun Ra declaiming to the audience. Unlike most such events, this is not over the band's vamping. Rather we have his pronouncements unaccompanied, with the band responding to them in rather free ways. The result is highly theatrical, in the spirit of the *Black Mass* collaboration with Amiri Baraka.

Since the CD booklet has a complete transcription of the text, I won't dwell on the (somewhat familiar) details. The main note is a Nietzschean transvaluation of values. Ra claims that hell propaganda is designed to scare folks (especially black ones) from outer space. The "bottomless pit" really refers to the depths of space: hell "is an ancient name for the sun" (he's no doubt thinking of "helios" here). Sun Ra actually admits he is "black and part of the black race"—a position he typically denied and thus a tribute to the orbital pull of the Black Power movement even on the man from Saturn. His assurance that "[t]here's nothing that can stop black people from having their own government" secures Ra's place in the tradition of liberatory black nationalism alongside other such luminaries as Marcus Garvey and Malcolm X. Finally, Sun Ra explains the decline of black folks from their Egyptian pyramid-building heyday along Gnostic lines: they have "neglected ... the creator of the universe" in favor of a lesser deity, "the white man."

This epic exegesis is followed by a trumpet and percussion interlude, more percussion and a blasting Moog synthesizer solo that thoroughly investigates the instrument and takes the audience into outer space. Some comfort is provided for the bewildered by a soothing delivery of "The Satellites Are Spinning" which underscores by background chanting that the Arkestra's ultimate goal here is to "abolish sorrow."

The second disk is even more esoteric: it's a tape of Sun Ra's third class in a course he taught at UC Berkeley in the spring of 1971 (a month before the concert on disk one). Known as "Sun Ra 171" or "The Black Man in the Cosmos," this course accommodated both students taking it for credit and local folks who wanted to sit in. John Szwed's biography goes into detail on its depth and rigor (Sun Ra after all had some training as a teacher). But an actual audio document from it is revelatory. Ra had both a message and a method: his message, as one might expect was a threefold project of 1) reminding African Americans of their glorious past; 2) confronting them with their hideously debased present; and 3) helping them toward a glorious future which involved not just Black Power and empowerment (economic and political), but ultimately moving into outer space.

His method was cultural deprogramming and reprogramming: both a matter of directing his audience to esoteric readings and his cross-lingual deconstruction of etymologies—for he believed, as did William Burroughs and many others (any linguist?), that language is the primary means of control and concealment for the powers that be. Hence, for example, "human" suggests both "hue-man" (the color factor) and "hew-man" (mortality, our inevitable date with the Grim Reaper). Or consider the connection between "sins" and "sense" and "cents." Ra believed that one had to confront and acknowledge one's own evil as well as good to be honest about the human condition and to survive in and profit from life—once again, more than a whiff of Nietzsche who mistrusted Christianity as a slave religion. For him, the message of the Book of Job is to "drop your righteousness and you'll get everything you want."

As the audience's appreciative laughter suggests, Sun Ra was an entertaining lecturer. He would allow for a question and answer period to interact with his students. And for the record, here he claims he is "not a human being"—a month before the concert where he says he is "part of the black race." So clearly there was some waffling going on, as well as the strong siren call of the Black Power movement at Berkeley and the Black Panther party. Sun Ra not only taught here; he was transformed by what he experienced as well (if only momentarily).

Intergalactic Research, the second "Lost Reel," combines two shows: a summer 1971 performance at Berkeley's Native Son club (around the time of the material documented in the first of this series) and an unknown location from 1972. The Native Son gig is on the cusp of the European tour that featured concerts like the Helsinki date: that band at that level of proficiency. The sound is very experimental, to say the least, with plenty of wailing skronk from both Allen's alto and whoever was on baritone sax. The themes from the lectures recur in the space chants. On "Why Go to the Moon?," the band adds "try Sun Ra" and "be your natural self." There's also some nice loopy synthesizer work from the maestro and a delicate interchange between the *kora* and the bass.

The second concert recording begins with another fine Moog solo, over which June Tyson eventually sings "Outer Space (Is a Pleasant Place)." A synth cascade of sound eventually leads to the band in free jazz mode both blowing simultaneously and taking solos—with further full band interjections (the sound of a crowded zoo burning down!). Ra's piano lead into the title track calms things down. "Intergalactic Research" also features a fine tenor showcase for John Gilmore. Given its repetitiousness, one suspects that this rare piece is probably in the "Discipline" series (which favors repetition)—and a very good example of same at that.

Volume three, *The Shadows Took Shape*, has two disks worth of an early 1970's concert labeled only "Spacemaster Concert." This excellently pristine recording is aptly named, for it begins with the full band blowing free jazz which morphs via a percussion break into a long solo on the electronic keyboards. After a while the Arkestra adds lyric-less chanting with an Egyptian melodic inflection: think of the soundtrack music for a film like *Land of the Pharaohs*. Sun Ra responds with muted synth overlays.

This improvisation is followed by a jaunty "Stardust from Tomorrow" and an extended reading of "Exotic Forest." This piece is the auditory equivalent of a Henri Rousseau painting or the sound of a giant progress through a jungle by a slow-moving army with elephants out of the *Mahābhārata*! Its plodding, steady beat is utterly hypnotic; a splendid trumpet solo adds some flair before the big percussion climax and the soft piano denouement.

The second disk begins with extended full-band fury lead-footing it on the space key; a little electric guitar at the end extends a hand to the rock audience before tranquility is restored with piano and bells. The space chants urge us to "[p]repare for the journey to other worlds ... . You better get ready for outer space," A previously unheard Ra poem recited by June Tyson to electronic keyboard accompaniment gives this release its title before we get another rhythmically driven number, "Friendly Galaxy." This last has an otherworldly synthesizer solo (an unusual setting) before a percussion break and a close on the "Watusi" theme.

Volume four, *Dance of the Living Image*, is another rehearsal tape from San Francisco, December 1974. Arkestra members have praised the rehearsals as often having better music than the concerts, and Sun Ra was known to have released some rehearsal sessions on the El Saturn label. So, as this music demonstrates, such material is worth putting out there. There are numerous treats on the first disk: a cocktail-lounge version of the theme from "Discipline 27-II" (listed as "unidentified title" for track 2), an oddly dissonant cover of "Sometimes I'm Happy" and a funky original with a big baritone sound and a spacious trumpet solo. But the highlight is unquestionably another original, an exotic yet tuneful processional that sounds like a fusion of Miles Davis' work in the *Sketches of Spain* era with his later electronic space funk (replete with guitar), one style evolving into another. A real gem of a rarity, in short.

The first half of the second disk involves Sun Ra showing the band a 1924 Charles L. Bates tune, "Hard Hearted Hannah." They first learn a Latin beat instrumental arrangement; then he teaches them the over-the-top lyrics, which crack the band up initially before they perfect the necessary deadpan delivery: "I saw Hard Hearted Hanna pour some water on a drowning man ... . Hard Hearted Hannah just love to see men suffer / Life is tough, but with Hard Hearted Hannah it's tougher."

The proceedings get even sillier with a Ra (very) original, an ode to flatulence which the compilers have called "Passin' Gas": "When you eat, don't eat too fast / Or you'll make music with your ass." This clear proof of Ra's deeply terrestrial humor was probably too outre even for the Arkestra to deliver in live performance. (The farting backup vocals are also quite special.) And then, turning on a dime, a straight and lovely run-through of Duke Ellington's "Sophisticated Lady" (except for some work on the ending and the vocals after the initial pass). In rehearsal as well as in concert, Sun Ra likes variety and the shock value of abrupt transitions. The tape ends with a version of the "Watusi" riff arranged just for the horns, reeds and flutes.

The Universe Sent Me, Lost Reel Collection Volume Five, presents excerpts from two concerts in the early 1970s. The first, a 1972 outdoor performance at the South Street Seaport Museum in New York City, is chiefly distinguished by an early, lush instrumental-only rendering of "Discipline 27-II." The subdued conclusion is probably as quiet as the Arkestra ever got, especially in the early 1970s—and indeed previously in the set there's lots of more characteristic free-blowing full-band space key and solo skronk.

The second show is from Paris a year and several months later. The microphone placement is near the reeds and horns, so they come through with exceptional clarity. But the vocals are muddy, which is not initially a problem since the declamations over "Discipline 27-II" (again) are also available in clearer form on the Club Lingerie tapes (Audio Series Volume Two; see above). It's worth straining to hear the rap over the improvisation in the latter part of the show, however. It's a rare recording of a legendary rant John Szwed refers to in his Ra biography (258): "Anyone can give up their life. Why don't you give up your death? ... I require you to give up your life and to give up your death." I guess that's the only way to enter the impossible world of Sun Ra's mythocracy: to go beyond life AND death. He's clearly holding his own with Philip K. Dick (check out his recently published *Exegesis!*) and / or the Gnostics here ... .

The sixth (and last as of this writing) Lost Reel is *The Road to Destiny*, an October 18, 1973 date at the Gibus in Paris (not the same music as on the other Gibus CD discussed above). Arkestra drummer "Bugs" Hunter made the recording. As he turns the tape on, he pronounces "Arkestra" with a short "e": "Erkestra." (Irkestra?!) A puzzling moment probably attributable to a regional accent. Highlights of the actual concert include an "Astro Black" that ends with "space ethnic voices": the women singing at the top of their vocal register without actually screaming (it sounds more like a very high-pitched rasp). We also get a very mellow reading of "Discipline 27" with a shimmering vibes effect on the electronic keyboards. "Discipline 27-II" features a very long cosmo-drama dialogue between Sun Ra and June Tyson (which also has a "give up your death" moment—not surprising given the proximity in date to the Paris show on Volume Five). The Arkestra throws in a repeated quotation of the main motif from John Coltrane's "A Love Supreme" on top of the "Discipline" theme. A final treat is the inclusion of the spiritual "Swing Low, Sweet Chariot" among the space chants. The vocal approach is whimsically retro: think of how the slaves would sing in a 1930s Hollywood film about the antebellum south. If Al Jolson did this, it would be racist; coming from the Arkestra, it's a loaded deconstruction of black "identity."

To turn from Transparency's abundant offerings, the most recent Sun

Ra rarities release (2013) is from England's Fantastic Voyage oldies label. *A Space Odyssey: From Birmingham to the Big Apple—The Quest Begins*. According to its compiler and annotator Kris Needs, this ambitious three CD package is a "tribute and beginner's guide" to Ra. It certainly is the former; but I think it would prove the latter for only a select and unusual demographic. The first disk, "Pre-Flight," assembles a generous amount of Sun Ra's pre-and / or-non Arkestra activities. The tracks include the ultra-rare: Clarence Williams and His Orchestra performing in 1933 "Chocolate Avenue," a composition then-teenage Ra mailed him—as such, the earliest recording of a Ra piece. (It's mainstream thirties Big Band writing with little indication of what's to come.) There's also a memorably catchy novelty record Ra arranged for bandleader Red Saunders (for the "race records" Okeh label) called "Hambone" after the technique African Americans developed for using the body as a percussion instrument. There's lots of other good stuff as well, about forty per cent of which is available on other compact disks from Evidence and Unheard Music. But this is a convenient if highly specialized compendium far more likely to interest diehard fans.

The other two disks, "Lift-Off" and "Future Shock" document the early days of the Arkestra in Chicago up to the cusp of their New York sojourn. Everything here is available elsewhere, but to my ears the sound is more pristine than on the Evidence reissues. As such, it's a pleasant enough selection of early releases showcasing his instrumental avant-garde jazz exotica in a way that helps you appreciate the rapid growth curve of the band in this era. Another interesting move here is to sequence eight compositions that appeared in diverse places as "A Suite of Philosophical Sounds," a longer work comprised of these shorter pieces which Sun Ra referred to in his notes. The anthology appropriately culminates with "The Beginning," a turning point on *The Futuristic Sounds of Sun Ra* discussed above.

One senses that Needs—who writes highly detailed and helpful liner notes —may be planning to continue this chronological project, which could make Fantastic Voyage a sixth label deeply invested in Sun Ra's work. The historical approach, which I have also tried to use here to some extent, is helpful given that Ra offers, as Kris Needs notes, "one of the world's most impossibly-convoluted [sic] discographies" (e.g. recordings released many years after they were made by Impulse records and the El Saturn label itself). This series if continued might truly be a good "beginner's guide" from which one could branch off into many interesting tangents based upon listening taste.

Tributes

And, as in the case of the death of Frank Zappa, a number of tribute CDs covering and / or honoring Ra appeared and continue to appear. The most important of these was *A Song for the Sun* (1999, El Ra Records), the first Arkestra release after the demise of their leader. The band uses the opportunity to unveil several previously unheard Ra compositions. The most beguiling of these is "They're Peepin'," a ditty of extraterrestrial voyeurism co-written with Allen: "They're peepin' in / They're doing it again." Space ethnic vocalist Art Jenkins adds his characteristic zaniness, and the band levitates (as it also does on "Cosmic Hop," an Allen composition that shows how closely he paid attention to Ra's lessons). "Blue Set" is another Ra blues piece that's nice to hear, but no great revelation. The rest of the CD mixes standards ("The Way You Look Tonight," a pointed and poignant "There Will Never Be Another You") with tributes to Ra ("Song for the Sun," "Watch the Sunshine," "Spread Your Wings") and new compositions in the style of Ra ("Galactic Voyage"). Respectfully, the Arkestra leaves the keyboard spot vacant to remind the listener who's absent as well as who abides.

Music for the 21st Century (2003, El Ra Records) is a live date from the Uncool Festival in Poschiavo, Switzerland. This recording shows how Marshall Allen learned to solve the two biggest problems of a post-Ra Arkestra: the lack of a keyboardist and the diminished uncanniness resultant from the lack of Ra's philosophical declamations to the audience. He compensates for the lack of electronic keyboards by extensive use of the EVI (Electronic Valve Instrument), a new windblown device that gives off the same timbres and loopy effects as a good synthesizer. And for the weirdness, he gives a lot of leash to the space vocalist Art Jenkins (now going by Arnold, it turns out). The result is not identical to Sun Ra's concerts, but something very much in the spirit of same (audio and visual methadone for the Ra junkie). Not for nothing is Sun Ra listed as "executive producer" on this release.

Marshall Allen's composition "Light and Darkness" has a nice hocketing introduction before it resolves into a theme. "Super Nova" offers us the triumphal return of Michael Ray on trumpet; Arnold Jenkins' space vocals grace "Voices from Outer Space." As John Szwed suggests in the liner notes, Allen's compositions hang together as a kind of suite in the spirit of Duke Ellington—which is why these somewhat elderly (in part) musicians play them straight through without a pause. "Blues Intergalactic" has a fine opening clarinet solo from Allen, and "Blue Sun" has lyrics worthy of Ra delivered by Jenkins: Today I saw a blue sun in the southwest corner of the sky ... I've never seen such beauty in a blue sun."

"In-B-Tween" has a nice vamp reminiscent of Ra's processionals over which Marshall Allen can deliver some free jazz skronk on his alto sax.

On "Mr. Mystery," Arnold Jenkins assures us that "Sun Ra left in a flying saucer": the beginning of the posthumous (and postmodern) Sun Ra mystery religion! After this, the first pause in the concert. A deep cut Ra cover follows ("Reflex Motion," not heard on any recording since 1962's *Secrets of the Sun*). "When You Wish Upon a Star" gives us an appropriate slice of Walt Disney to evoke the later incarnations and interests of the Arkestra when Ra was still on-planet. It's a jagged, edgy—and yet oddly moving—reading. As performed, the songs and its lyric have real resonance: "If your heart is in your dream / No request is too extreme." The concert appropriately ends with "We Travel the Spaceways," now a battle-scarred anthem for the band's strange celestial road. Allen's EVI's boops and blurps rev up the spaceship one more time to end the space memorial service as the extraterrestrial second line joyously comes back from the cemetery (which may contain an empty tomb).

The most recent release of the post-Ra Arkestra is a live date from the Paradox Music Club in Tilburg, the Netherlands, on June 20, 2008 (the last night of a five-day residency, released in 2009 on In and Out Records from Freiburg, Germany; I mention all this to indicate how the Arkestra is still all about finding supporters for temporary alliances rather than being regarded as the global cultural treasure they are and given a sinecure). This beautifully recorded set—my, how technology has advanced—is nicely balanced between four Sun Ra compositions (actually five, since there's a medley), four Marshall Allen pieces and a Fletcher Henderson cover. Arnold Jenkins and Michael Ray are not in attendance; but for the first time in fifteen years, the band has a keyboardist: Farid Barron on piano and organ. A wise decision, I think, since so many of Ra's works were designed to emphasize his keyboards.

The opener, Allen's "Space Walk," is a warm-up piece very similar to the improvisations that Sun Ra's band would play before he came out, a chance for the group to collectively stretch out. An instrumental "Discipline 27-II" follows (here called "27-B"; whatever) in medley with "I'll Wait for You." The former is instrumental only (no declamations, of course); the latter has group vocals and even some side excursions into other space chants ("This World Is Not My Home," "Angel Race"). Then we get more Ra originals: the deep cuts of the very early (1956) "Dreams Come True" (with a Knoel Scott vocal and a fine trumpet solo from Charles Davis) and "Velvet" (a driving instrumental from *Jazz in Silhouette* [1958] that ended up on the set list of some dates on the 1966 campus tour of the northeast).

"You'll Find Me" (Allen's instrumental rejoinder to Sun Ra's "I'll Wait for You"?) is a lovely, lyrical tune with an ear-catching piano solo from Barron. Appropriately, he does not try to sound like Sun Ra—nor could he, being more polished and less fiery. Allen's "Millennium" uses the full resources of the Arkestra in a big Cadillac arrangement to celebrate the new era and invite the audience to "come ride with us on cosmic dust." His "Take Off," given the title, is appropriately far out EVI-led electronica: the band at its spaciest. Then, just like Sun Ra used to do, Marshall Allen turns the band on a dime for a faithful reading of Ra mentor Fletcher Henderson's "Hocus Pocus." The recording ends with the hitherto-unreleased Sun Ra original "Space Idol," a boppy tune with an initial exploratory piano solo. No doubt there's much more of this quality in the vaults and notebooks of this astonishingly prolific musician.

But how much will we get to hear? *Points on a Space Age*, a 2009 documentary about the Marshall Allen Arkestra, directed by Ephraim Asili, is somewhat pessimistic. There really isn't anyone as qualified as Marshall Allen to carry on, and he's in his late eighties. Members see the current state of the band as the end of the line, even though there are young players joining it: it's a question of leadership.

This film (available on DVD) is a fine tribute to Sun Ra in its own right. It skillfully intercuts JFK speeches and NASA footage with archival films of Ra in Egypt and the contemporary band to establish the historical context for Ra's space-age agenda and mission. We hear from the Arkestra about diverse proclivities of their late leader: his wanting to vary the band with different personalities and skill levels to create a microcosm of the omniverse; his visiting electronic keyboard factories to show them what he wanted to hear from the instruments; his desire to appeal to all the senses in his shows (hence the strong visual element); and his interest in "moving orchestration" resulting in the performers moving through space as they played (cf. similar sonic interests on the part of Charles Ives and Edgard Varese). One band member describes what they play as "African American classical music." The most striking concert footage in the documentary shows us a dancer in a kind of trapeze cage lifted off the stage and executing an aerial ballet to "Love in Outer Space" while a psychedelic abstract film plays in the background.

In addition, Arkestra members have spun off into other solo projects. Most notably, trumpeter Michael Ray and the Cosmic Krewe showcase Ra material in their concerts and recordings. Ray and keyboardist Adam Klipple execute an especially delicate reading of the lesser-known "Island in Space" (now available in its original Ra version as "Island in the Sun" on *Janus*). Marshall Allen also led a quartet for several recordings with reedist Mark Whitecage, bassist Dominic Duval and drummer / Arkestra member Luqman Ali. As with John Gilmore's side outings, it's interesting to hear Allen playing in another context. Ra's spirit nevertheless presides understandably over some of their choice of standards ("When You Wish upon a Star," "Fly Me to the Moon"). The sensitive production values make these

CIMP (Creative Improvised Music Projects) releases well worth a listen.

Of the tribute albums by non-Arkestra personnel, *Wavelength Infinity* is the best (and even features a few cameos from Arkestra members). The players here don't really try to sound like Ra's band; they use the music to do their own (often unusual) thing. Steve Adams and Ben Goldberg's duet workout for reeds on "Transition" is spellbinding, as is The Residents' adaptation of "Space Is the Place." The Splatter Trio do much justice to bassist Ronnie Boykins' composition "Tiny Pyramids." Then there's "Miss Muragtroid" (Alicia J. Rose) accompanying her recitation of Ra's poem "Nature's Law" on accordion. The Residents, Miss Murgatroid and Eugene Chadbourne with Zappa alum / drummer Jimmy Carl Black (on another version of "Space Is the Place") all separately manage the enviable feat of playing cover versions of Ra stranger than the originals by the master. We also get an appropriately electronic version of "Disco 3000" from Elliot Sharp. But the absolute highlight of the double CD is a "Tri-School Artestra" of elementary school players performing "Planet Earth." The joyous simplicity and genuine wildness of the kids captures an element in Ra perfectly that the more adult and sophisticated Arkestra could only approximate. When they whisper "the spirit of Sun Ra" at the end, you can believe that Ra truly lives!

I am less enamored of *Spaceways Incorporated: Thirteen Cosmic Standards by Sun Ra and Funkadelic*. This tribute from reedist Ken Vandermark, bassist Nat McBride and drummer Hamid Drake has some fine original jamming on "El is a Sound of Joy" and "We Travel the Spaceways." It even has the blessing of the great Ra scholar John Corbett, who co-produced. (In fact, it illustrates the argument of his opening essay in *Extended Play* by gesturing toward a genealogy that links Ra with Funkadelic.) So what's my gripe? Only this: Ra was a teacher, first and foremost. And this set provides a misleading lesson to the novice jazz fan most likely to pick this up as an introduction to the material it covers. The Ra songs are quieter jazz numbers; the Funkadelic covers are loud, kicking funk. Why such a neat division of labor? There are plenty of loud funk jams in the Arkestra's late-seventies repertoire (and scads of loud Ra generally). Why make Ra the high-art chamber alternative to Funkadelic? It's a neat structure, but I fear it's also facile. I'd prefer the cosmic slop of the truth—which would establish the linkages even better.

I am much fonder of alt-rock band Yo La Tengo's one-off, 2002's *Nuclear War, Or How I Learned to Stop Worrying and Love the Bomb*. This CD offers four versions of Sun Ra's soulful Reagan-era agit-prop classic. The first version is a highly percussive but quite faithful reading of the original version's call-and-response vocals. The only change made is an addition of "neutron bombs" to the chanted arsenal (which I don't hear on the Arkestra versions). The second take adds didgeridoo and a spirited children's chorus (getting to cuss up a storm on the lyrics, including an opportunity to drop the "M" bomb). You can hear one kid softly chuckling at song's end.

Version three is a longer, jazzier take with piano and horns added to (again, as in take one) heavy percussion. The saxophonist throws out some free-jazz skronk in the spirit of the Arkestra; the trumpeter lights off some Michael Ray inspired flares. The jazz players sing and chant as well; one muses about the oddity of "walking around without an ass." And finally we get a techno remix of the second reading by Mike Ladd: four diverse ways of looking at the song for a tribute that's both respectful and irreverent—respectful to the irreverence of the material! Would Sun Ra want it any other way?

No doubt there will be more to come of Ra's music as reissues proceed, audience tapes surface and his music enters further into the repertoire of classic jazz. All likely developments, *pacé* Ken Burns. Meanwhile, there is plenty to listen to if you find earth boring.

Why Sun Ra Matters

The *Washington Post* obituary for Sun Ra, I recall, described him as "the missing link between Duke Ellington and Public Enemy." Although a glib soundbyte, it captures a certain truth about Ra. He was not only a collapser of all periods of music, though, from the ancient world to the space age; he was also a synchronic absorber of whatever was most interesting as a sonic possibility. Perhaps little that he did per se was truly unique: on that score, his greatest contribution might have been the addition of electronic keyboards to the Big Band ensemble. But the fusion of musical influences gave him an utterly remarkable sound that helped kick start post-bop jazz into all sorts of experimentation. (Some, like free jazz, partially arose from a misreading of the Ra project. Even mistaken apprehensions of the Arkestra proved fertile.) Who else combined dissonance, microtones, the bottom end of the orchestra so loved by Edgard Varese, electronics, playing chords on top of each other (the "space key"), the relentless polyrhythms of Africa, enough repetition to satisfy Phillip Glass or John Cage—plus costumes, dance, theater, spectacle? That was the live show; the recordings anticipated punk production with their avoidance of glitz and willingness to experiment with unusual techniques of recording. Before *White Light / White Heat*, there was *Art Forms of Dimensions Tomorrow*. And all delivered with precision and discipline. First and foremost as a musician and showman, Sun Ra carved out a special niche in American popular culture.

But as we have seen, Ra was also a poet and a philosopher. Although I have concentrated understandably upon his music and ideas, his poetic output also figures into his importance—even though it is as destined to be marginalized by literary anthologies as his jazz is from some flat-browed approaches to the tradition. It would strike many as not poetry at all because of its high level of abstraction. Like Ra's music, it is not necessarily trying to fit in with the conventions of its form.

But I would submit that Ra is not writing in a vacuum. His verse combines the aphorisms and parables of an eccentric American poet like Stephen Crane with the repetition and wordplay of a Gertrude Stein. Here is "The Foolish Foe," Sun Ra at his closest approach to Stephen Crane:

> There were some things I never tried to do
> And most of them were things I wanted to do
> ... There were opposing forces
> Why should they oppose me?
> Why? Why?
> Now and then I thought, there is
> No such enemy as I think they are.
> But then, it is beyond thought ... it is beyond thought
> I feel
> These opposing forces whose power is their weakness
> The power they grant to their servants / subjects
> They exist, Indeed they do.
> I feel and always have felt
> It is, it always was true
> Since this plane of existent I came to be, to know
> They are are/were here!
> I never resisted them,
> They think I did
> It was only pretense desires I projected to them
> Were my non-resistance weapon/shield of defense
> I do not desire what they thought I desire
> Neither now nor ever then
> Non-resistance became my resistance
> My resistance is non-resistance. Do they challenge?
> I resist the challenge
> Foolish foe!
> I have already won the victory
> How? You will never know.
> I have forgotten the how I did
> I only know I know only
> I only know ... .
> It was never your game,
> It is always mine
> I resist the challenge
> Foolish Foe
> I always win the victory
> You did not know the secret code
> If I win, I win and if I lose I win!
> You did not know
>
> You do not know! (Szwed 326-7)

Although longer and slightly more abstract than a typical Crane poem (and containing more Steinian grammatical perplexities and repetitions), "The Foolish Foe" can still bring to mind a Crane poem such as the following:

> Why do you strive for greatness, fool?
> Go pluck a bough and wear it.
> It is as sufficing.
>
> My Lord, there are certain barbarians
> Who tilt their noses
> As if the stars were flowers,
> And thy servant is lost among their shoe-buckles.
> Fain would I have mine eyes even with their eyes.
>
> Fool, go pluck a bough and wear it. (#52, Katz 56)

The archaic language is the main clue here that the above is by Stephen Crane and not Sun Ra. While there is little evidence to suggest Ra was necessarily exposed to Crane (or Stein, for that matter), these iconoclasts innovate in their verse in resonant ways.

A good example of Ra in a more Steinian voice can be found in his poem "Nature's Laws" ("Nature's Law" is the title given on the Miss Murgatroid version):

> According to nature's laws and laws
> I be as I am and what I am not even
> Because and yet not even because
> Because, for, and, that is ... . why ... .
> Because, should and why. If then
> Then and so
> Perhaps
> May
> If I do, I will
> And if I don't I won't
> Either way I do and don't perspectively
> Why, when, how, what, which
> Yes, no, neither. (Abraham 84)

Any random sample of Gertrude Stein's writing will show parallel interests in repetition as a way to restore to words their uncanniness. I open *The Heath Anthology of American Literature, Volume 2,* to the following excerpt from Stein's *Geographical History of America*:

> *Page III*
> Human nature has nothing to do with it.

> Human nature.
> Has nothing to do with it.
>
> *Page IV*
>
> Emptying and filling an ocean has nothing to do with it because
> if
>   it is full it is an ocean and if it is empty it is not an ocean.
> Filling and emptying an ocean has nothing to do with it.
>
> *Page IV*
>
> Nothing to do with master-pieces.
>
> *Page V*
>
> Nothing to do with war. (1261-2)

Und so weiter. You get the general resemblance, I trust!

Sun Ra used his poetic writing to illustrate his cosmology and to aid in deprogramming his audience from its mistakenly earthbound and death-oriented ways. It was a teaching tool, in short, as was his music. The published poetry often overlaps with the song lyrics, as in the case of "In Some Far Place" (which became the lyrics for the song / space chant "I'll Wait for You"):

> In some far place
> Many light years in space
> I'll wait for you.
> Where human feet have never trod ... .
> Where human eyes have never seen,
> I'll build a world of abstract dreams
> And wait for you.
>
> In tomorrow's realm
> We'll take the helm
> Of a new ship ... .
> Like the lash of a whip
> We'll be suddenly on the way
> And lightning-journey
> To yet another other friendly shore. (Abraham 31)

The whip simile is an unusually poetic touch for Ra, and recalls his threats to chain up black people and drag them into outer space (in the film *Space Is The Place*). Ra saw himself as a revisionist slave master. Whereas the white slavers disciplined their charges to dehumanizing ends, Ra's disciplinary regime will ultimately liberate his followers from the deathly ways of earth. Through music, drama and words he offered this charismatic promise.

Sun Ra was also of some interest and importance as an amateur street-corner philosopher and sage. Consider his unusual philosophical position, as helpfully unpacked by John Szwed in the biography. Ra's beliefs were an unusual, but not unprecedented, fusion of Nietzschean iconoclasm and platonic idealism. On the one hand, Ra attacked the same targets as Nietzsche: Christianity and democracy. The way of the cross and an overemphasis upon freedom were gross misapprehensions to him. Like Nietzsche, Ra was a transvaluer of such fundamental western assumptions. He preferred Egyptian discipline and leadership (as he perceived it) to Christianity's slave religion which turned the other cheek; he preferred enlightened autocracy (or his preferred term, mythocracy) to the illusory freedom of democracy that gave the incompetent the same access to power as the enlightened pharaoh leader.

But he also preserved some absolute values from his skeptical transvaluations, however inexplicitly he evoked them: "beauty, discipline, space, the Creator, infinity" (Szwed 383-4). There were absolute values in the universe that offered connections to an ideal world of beauty as in the writings of Plato and Pythagoras. His reconciliation of these two positions was simply that these values were not the values of earth. Ra hop-scotched over Christianity, St. Paul and the enlightenment itself to offer a fusion of ancient Greece and Egypt with a pisgah view of the cosmos.

Curiously enough, this reconciliation of Plato and Nietzsche was done before, by the German philosopher Max Scheler in his 1914 treatise *Der Formalismus in der Ethik und die Materiale Wertethik* (roughly translatable as "Formalism in Ethics and the Material Ethics of Values"). This work has never been translated into English, so it is unlikely Ra was ever exposed to it. But Scheler's project, which came to be known as "ethical platonism," was independently charting the same northwest passage between Plato and Nietzsche that so interested Sun Ra. A final curiosity here is that Pope John Paul II's theological scholarship prior to his papacy concentrated upon Scheler, ethical platonism and the issues it raised. No doubt Ra would have been mightily amused by these ironies![9]

Besides Sun Ra's importance as a musician, showman, poet and philosopher, he deserves some credit for having "kept the sixties going a long time," as John Sinclair has observed (in Szwed 354). Ra's musical commune of musicians, charismatic playfulness, and obliging fusion of experimentation and joy were the very best of what the sixties had to offer culturally and existentially. For most of us, this experience was a brief epiphany before things went sour. But Ra kept the soap bubble up in the air for three decades: for this alone he deserves much credit.

Nonetheless, Sun Ra genially saw himself as a failure, albeit a "successful" one:

> I did never want to be successful. I want to be the only thing
> I could be without anyone stopping me in America—that is, to
> be a failure. So I feel pretty good about it, I'm a total failure ...
> . So now as I've been successful as a failure, I can be successful.
> (Szwed 366)

There is much to be said about his observations. He is addressing the ultimate separation of art and commerce in America. If you choose the path of art, you will in all likelihood be an economic failure. Ra's remarks are a typical transvaluation of these considerations. If the sentence of Earth is one of death, America's is one of failure for the artist who refuses to compromise. That might be Earth's sentence as well, for what country really supports its artists? Where is arcadia? When was the golden age?

These comments also underline Ra's connection with the sixties; as we all know, that too was a "successful failure." It accomplished some goals regarding civil rights and ending the war in Vietnam, but it fell far short of its expectations.

In the packaging for *Blue Delight* (1988), Sun Ra included a valedictory poem for his audience:

> We are approaching the twin roads of the future,
> One day planet earth must choose to change;
> And you must choose
> There is no other way.
> Don't forget the alter hints I give to you ...
> One day, you must choose to change
> Be sure your intuition's voice is not defied
> Or perhaps neglectfully denied.
> No other voice will speak to you
> No other voice knows what to say. ("You Must Choose")

Ra's confidences to the reader / listener ally him with that most intimate of nineteenth-century American poets, Walt Whitman. In 1855, Whitman ended "Song of Myself" with this assurance:

> Failing to fetch me at first keep encouraged,
> Missing me one place search another,
> I stop somewhere waiting for you. (89)

Whereas Whitman advised us to look for him under our boot-soles, Ra's promise of future rendezvous is celestial and intergalactic: in some far place, many light-years in space, he waits for us.

So much for Sun Ra's universal message and significance. I want to conclude by briefly addressing his specific importance for African American culture. For like many artifacts of same culture, Sun Ra's work was double-coded: it had a universal message and a specifically targeted meaning for black audiences. I am not saying anything new here. Graham Lock in his liner notes to *Live in London 1990* (with the help of Victor Schonfield, John Szwed and Julian Vein) makes the same point. I would only add a critical concept by way of a prelude from Henry Louis Gates, Jr. In his seminal work *The Signifying Monkey*, Gates notes how African American texts are unusually intertextual: they bounce off each other in two distinct ways which he calls "unmotivated" and "motivated" signifying. Unmotivated signifying is done in homage to a preceding text (he uses the example of Alice Walker's recycling of tropes from Zora Neale Hurston). Motivated signifying offers a critique of the earlier text: it is a parody, not a homage or a pastiche (Gates 346).

Although Lock does not use this terminology, he astutely discovered that Sun Ra was deep into motivated signifying on several counts. For starters, his use of Egypt as a cultural touchstone turns on its head the standard identification in the spirituals of African Americans with the Israelites (e.g., "Go Down Moses"). Along Nietzschean lines, Ra perceived that such a linkage was disempowering: why be slaves when you are descended from pharaohs? The sorrow songs' vehicle of escape was a "sweet chariot coming for to carry [them] home" (and indeed, as we have seen, the Arkestra would even include this in the space chants sometimes). But Ra's vehicles of preference were moonships, rockets, flying saucers. And his goal was not heaven, but outer space: "pluto too"—and beyond (Lock).

All this Graham Lock correctly observes. I'd add a few more examples of motivated signifying upon spirituals and the black church. Where this body puts its ultimate faith in the suffering Jesus, Sun Ra countered with himself as a "living myth" who even had aspects of Lucifer in him. Sun Ra was very interested in the Creator, but he had a profound distrust of the Son (vs. the SUN!) as a bad example of suffering and passive endurance of the world's woes. Lucifer's rebellion was a more useful role model. (In this respect, Ra is solidly in the earlier, more European Romantic tradition alongside William Blake, Lord Byron, Walt Whitman and many others).

And lastly, Sun Ra trumped the alienation expressed in many spirituals ("sometimes I feel like a motherless child") with a far more profound distancing claim: "this *world* is not my home" (italics mine). The problem was not being black; it was being human, terrestrial. The solution was to transcend the human and discover one's inner alien—and join other beings in the omniverse.

Considered in this light, Sun Ra offered a major alternative to his people through his lyrics, music, and writings. He offered a space-age version of black power that can be profitably compared with the labors of a Marcus

Garvey or a Malcolm X. Like the former, he by his own admission was "a total failure" (Szwed 366 again). His program never caught on as a mass movement; it was embraced only by a few fans and band members—and they're / we're not getting any younger! It is gratifying to note that some younger listeners are discovering this enticing singularity in our cultural cosmos (and I hope this chapter piques some further interest in Sun Ra for the reader). In this regard as well, he waits as an alternative for anyone who "find[s] Earth boring." Or worse ... .

Notes and Works Cited

Notes

[1] In addition to the singles collection on the Evidence label, there are three other CD compilations of Ra's non-Arkestra doo wop and vocal group arrangements. The most efficient collection for the curious is John Corbett's *Spaceship Lullaby* on his Unheard Music label. You get some interesting original compositions such as "Chicago USA," his sonic tribute to the Windy City reminiscent of some of Charles Ives's urban sound paintings, as well as the sublime corn of some inspired covers. The Nu Sounds version of "Stranger in Paradise" really takes off when the lyrics approach pianist / arranger Sun Ra's interests: "somewhere in space / I hang suspended." (Cf. "Just One of Those Things" with its"trip to the moon on gossamer wings.") "Holiday for Strings" is given a manic treatment with resultant amusement for the listener—surpassed only by the toy romance of "The Wooden Soldier and the China Doll." Clearly Ra's tastes are thoroughly eclectic: he can hear something of interest in schmaltz even Lawrence Welk might have taken a pass on.

This compilation features, in addition to the Nu Sounds and the Cosmic Rays, the thoroughly unwashed Lintels, a street corner doo wop group not afraid to croon, "you my only love."

[2] See Dan Noel's fascinating book *Approaching Earth* for a Jungian interpretation of why our culture, including Ra, would be so compelled to link the space-age with antiquity. Stanley Kubrick's *2001: A Space Odyssey* is as obvious an illustration of this habit of mind as the oeuvre of Sun Ra.

[3] Sun Ra was also an angel and a devil as well as an alien. He explained his lifelong celibacy by citing Matthew 22:30 ("They neither marry nor

are given in marriage but are like angels that shine forth like the sun" [in Szwed 347]). Ra's biographers have speculated more pragmatically that it had something to do with his nearly lifelong untreated hernia (cf. Henry James's "obscure wound"). Ra's death is linked to its operative repair without anyone's consent when he was being treated for pneumonia in Alabama (Corbett 174).

As for his status as demon, consider that Ra made the doo-wop groups he worked with in Chicago call him "Lucifer": "That was the only name he would have us call him. Even after a year when he changed to Sun Ra we still called him Lucifer" (Szwed 91). As late as 1982 he kept that name; he issued an album called *A Fireside Chat with Lucifer*. Alien, angel, devil: Ra wanted to hog all corners of the Greimasian semiotic square except human!

[4] Art Jenkins had been in the Arkestra since 1962's *Secrets of the Sun*. He wanted to join the band as a vocalist, but was told by Ra that the band needed a singer who could deliver the impossible: "The possible has been tried and failed; now I want to try the impossible." After many unsuccessful attempts at fitting in using various effects, Jenkins finally succeeded when he sang into a ram's horn backwards and manipulated the little opening with his hand. Ra laughed, "Now that's impossible!"—and Jenkins joined the Arkestra (Szwed, *Space* 192-3). "Solar Differentials" off *Secrets of the Sun* is the first example of this material; the Judson Hall concert shows that Jenkins was getting ever more adept at this technique!

[5] A strange personage known as "The Good Doctor" delivered to the ESP label a third lost volume of these 1965 sessions, resulting in the 2005 release of *Heliocentric Worlds Volume 3: The Lost Tapes*. If you like this era and approach (avant-garde chamber jazz instrumentals), you'll want to listen to this as well if only for one long seventeen-minute track: "Intercosmosis." Like "Cosmic Chaos" on volume two, it features an epic battle royal in its mid-section between Pat Patrick (baritone sax), John Gilmore (tenor) and Marshall Allen (alto). The first third of the piece is a Patrick solo; the last third is a more meditative and subdued interplay between Ra on piano and Ronnie Boykins on arco bass. As in much of the work from this era, the Arkestra is doing some sound-painting on a very large canvas. If "Intercosmosis" were a painting, it would be a Jackson Pollock or a Mark Rothko—guaranteed to take any open-eared listener on an epic space journey!

[6] In fact, avant-popist Beefheart's relationship with major labels provides a good parallel with Ra's misadventures. Both innovators were equally hot potatoes in the culture industry.

[7]More recently, the Transparency label has released *The Sun Ra All Stars*, four pre-Montreux European dates for this amazing ensemble on five discs. The first two discs cover an October 27, 1983 show in Milan. The opening improvisation features careful dialogue and exploration before exploding into a climax of free-jazz soloing. The next piece has fine piano-reeds-drums and percussion interplay before the trumpets kick in; Archie Shepp's tenor solo is a standout. The closing percussive interaction segues into a driving, simple yet dramatic bass figure from Richard Davis that eventually draws the ensemble in for some serious cooking. After all this improvisation, Don Cherry adds a lush vocal to Sun Ra's equally opulent piano and Davis' walking bass lines on the "sun" standard "East of the Sun"—which leads to even more retro ragtime piano work on "King Porter Stomp."

The second disk reminds us why this band was called the Sun Ra All Stars. Their repertoire consisted of group improvisations, jazz standards and Sun Ra compositions. Although the other members of the group had written a lot of music in their own right, this was Ra's show: he was the master of ceremonies. So we get a lovely reading of "What's New?" with more lovely bass work (bowing, soloing, interacting with the percussion section) and a mutated "Cocktails for Two" (because of Marshall Allen's alto skronk). Then two Ra originals conclude the show. "Spontaneous Simplicity" gets enhanced by a trumpet solo from Lester Bowie and Archie Shepp's full-bodied tenor sax. And finally, a highly polyrhythmic "Space Is the Place": after all, this band had three master drummers / percussionists (Famoudou Don Moye, Philly Joe Jones and Clifford Jarvis) and an astonishing bassist. Small wonder the former keep soloing after the piece ends.

The next day they opened their performance at the Zurich Jazz Festival with an improvisation that began with martial drumming and arco bass, followed by a soaring soprano sax solo from Archie Shepp and attentive percussion dialogue leading up to a Philly Joe Jones drum solo. Then Sun Ra played a piano solo, lyrical and pounding by turns, with trumpet grace notes in the background from Don Cherry. This eventually evolved into a barrelhouse blues with witty flourishes from trumpeter Lester Bowie. The highlight of the set from the standpoint of a Sun Ra follower would be their reverential and skillful reading of his standout composition "Lights on a Satellite." I would argue that this band performed the piece best of the many available recorded versions—a result of a jazz super-group instead of the always motley character of the Arkestra which mixed the old pros with rougher younger players in training. Not a false note here.

Then the show closes with some standards: again "What's New?" (its extended piano introduction eventually augmented by bass and drums and solid reed work) and "Cocktails for Two" (another "drunken" playful version courtesy of the reeds). The set concludes with "Poinciana," a piece they must have enjoyed playing since they also did long versions of it at the next two dates. As they should have. Not only does the tune have a lovely melody (which is why so many crooners [e.g., Frank Sinatra] have covered it), but the solo work showcases the diversity of the group—from the lyrical approaches of Shepp and Cherry to the subversions of Bowie. Richard Davis contributes an exquisite and multifaceted bass solo before the percussion section lands the spaceship with their subtle rhythmic conversations.

The Berlin concert (like the Paris show on the fifth disc) suffers from some inferior audio quality (more pronounced tape hiss). But in both cases, it's worth getting past that (and some receiver technologies can compensate for it). The Berlin show is also on DVD and discussed as such later. It opens with "Stars That Shine Darkly," a mostly free jazz romp with emerging climactic be-bop reed and trumpet work. The loose jam that follows is highlighted by Lester Bowie interpolating the New Orleans classic "Big Chief" (by E. Gaines). Bowie also throws a little "Rockin' Robin" at the end of the Ra composition "Somewhere Else." Then we get "Early Morning Blues" from Ra, with "laughing" reed and horn effects and a wacky Don Cherry vocal: "It's early in the morning / and I ain't got nothing but the blues / SUN RA."

Another fine reading of "Poinciana" ensues, featuring great tenor variations on the theme from John Gilmore. At the end of the interpretation, we transition from synthesizer to drum soloing and a quiet percussion break segueing into an unusual "Shadow World": after the head, we get synthesizer, piano, trumpet and walking bass, gong and didgeridoo (the Australian aboriginal drone tube, courtesy of Don Moye), trumpet and reed—all before extensive power drumming ("at the edge of magic," percussionist and Grateful Dead member Mickey Hart would say). Philly Joe Jones, Clifford Jarvis and Don Moye engage in a three-way cutting contest which includes some serious cymbal play. The following jam that ends the tape moves the Battle Royal over to the reed section which gets its skronky wailing on. The Germans loved every second of it as perennial supporters of Sun Ra and all his works.

The Paris concert (which concludes the collection, but not the tour) is the one where they really push the envelope—a combination of playing together for three previous shows, then having two days off? One thing this ensemble did share with the Arkestra's approach was an inclination to play the adventurous improvisatory stuff (in part) as a lead-in to the standards (including Ra's own older compositions). By Sun Ra's own admission with respect to the Arkestra, this was a prophylactic gesture designed to clear the house of any closed-eared individuals who wouldn't give the band their absolute commitment. So it is here with the didgeridoo leading the way. The second improvisation has a bowed bass introduction, Archie Shepp running some bop scales, Ra's reeds wailing, a percussion interlude, some sensitive dialogue between bassist Davis and trumpeter Lester Bowie and even more intense reed wailing from Marshall Allen on alto sax to wrap it up. Then it's on to the standards ... .

Sun Ra takes us once again "Over the Rainbow" on piano (with occasional thunderous cascades of sound) abetted by Don Cherry's trumpet and Archie Shepp's sax. The first big surprise is a completely against-the-grain (but equally brilliant) reading of Ra's "Lights on a Satellite." Where the Zurich version was an utter realization of the score's intentions (what the Arkestra tried to do fully delivered), this reading is relentlessly against the grain: a sonic deconstruction that moves the margins of the piece to the center. For starters, it's done to a calypso beat and the melody gets drowned out by bursts of responsive sound. Much of the time only one player is holding down the melody line—and even then, messing with that in some way (the bassist fiddling with the duration of the notes and the tempo). The mocking interrupters remind me, oddly enough. of the responding instruments in Charles Ives's "The Unanswered Question."

A loose and upbeat "What's New?" follows. One is reminded that this can be a sad and wistful evocation of lost love (the way Linda Ronstadt / Frank Sinatra and Nelson Riddle's orchestra deliver it, for example). But not here: it's either just a musical text or all is forgiven in the unsung lyrics (how ya doing, ex-love?). We get alternating energetic solos from Bowie, Davis, Shepp and Jones. The performance of "Poinciana" is also against the grain of the Zurich and Berlin readings. After the piano statement of the theme, Sun Ra solos on organ; Don Cherry gives us full-throttle trumpet; Lester Bowie slides in a quotation from "Tropical Heat Wave"; little instruments give us a Spanish flair; the didgeridoo shows up one more time. Then Ra restates the theme on a wild synthesizer setting (think Keith Emerson's approach to the conclusion of "Lucky Man"!). Another standard transformed, even from this band's previous takes on it.

The Sun Ra All Stars conclude by rewarding the persistent conservative listeners for hearing all this avant-garde stretching with a straight-up version of "'Round Midnight." John Gilmore's closing tenor solo brings us back to Earth after an amazing ride. As you might be gathering, this is some astonishing music.

[8]The obvious exception being *A Black Mass*, the Arkestra's collaboration with Amiri Baraka.

[9]I am grateful to my German colleague Rod Taylor for these helpful insights.

Works Cited

Abraham, Adam, ed. *Sun Ra Collected Works Volume I: Immeasurable Equation.* Chandler, Arizona: Phaelos, 2005.

Blumenthal, Bob. Liner notes for *Sun Ra & his Arkestra Live at Montreux.* Inner City 1039. 1976.

Campbell, Robert L. Liner notes for *The Great Lost Sun Ra Albums.* Evidence 22217-2. 2000.

———. Liner notes for *The Singles.* Evidence 22164-2. 1996.

Carles, Philippe. Liner notes for *Unity.* Horo HDP 19-20. 1978.

Cassenti, Frank, director. *Mystery, Mr. Ra: Sun Ra and his Arkestra.* Rhapsody Films, distributor. 1984.

Corbett, John. *Extended Play: Sounding Off from John Cage to Dr. Funkenstein.* Durham, NC: Duke University Press, 1994.

Gates, Henry Louis, Jr. "Introduction to *The Signifying Monkey.*" In *African American Literary Theory: A Reader.* Ed. Winston Napier. New York: NYU Press, 2000. Pages 339-347.

Gershon, Pete."Twenty First Century Music: Reissues, Memorabilia & the Ongoing Activities of the Sun Ra Arkestra Under the Direction of Alto Saxaphonist Marshall Allen." In *Sun Ra: Interviews and Essays.* Ed. John Sinclair. London: Headpress, 2010.

Katz, Joseph, ed. *The Complete Poems of Stephen Crane.* Ithaca, NY: Cornell University Press, 1972.

Keel, John. *Visitors from Space: The Astonishing, True Story of the Mothman Prophecies.* St. Albans, Great Britain: Panther, 1976.

Lange, Art. Liner notes for *We Travel the Spaceways / Bad and Beautiful.* Evidence 22038-2. 1992.

Lauter, Paul, general editor. *The Heath Anthology of American Literature: Volume Two.* Third edition. Boston: Houghton Mifflin, 1998.

Lock, Graham. Liner notes for *Live in London 1990.* Blast First BFFP60 CD. 1996.

Meltzer, David, ed. *Writing Jazz.* San Francisco: Mercury House, 1999.

Michel, Ed. Liner notes for *The Great Lost Sun Ra Albums.* Evidence 22217-2. 2000.

Ra, Sun. *The Ark and the Ankh: Sun Ra / Henry Dumas in Conversation 1966, Slug's Saloon NYC.* IKEF02. 2001.

———. *The Immeasurable Equation.* Xerox of collected edition compiled by Hartmut Geerken, courtesy of BenWa.

———. Liner notes for *When Angels Speak of Love.* Evidence 22216-2. 2000.

———. "You Must Choose." In liner notes for *Blue Delight.* A&M 5260. 1989.

Rammel, Hal. Liner notes for *Strange Strings.* 1966. Unheard Music Series ALP263CD. Ca. 2006.

Rose, Cynthia. *Living in America: The Soul Saga of James Brown*. London: Serpent's Tail, 1990.
Schuller, Gunther and Martin Williams. Booklet essay for *Big Band Jazz: From the Beginnings to the Fifties*. Washington, DC: Smithsonian, 1983.
Shore, Michael. Liner notes for *Atlantis*. Evidence 22067-2. 1993.
Smith, R.J. *The One: The Life and Music of James Brown*. New York: Gotham Books, 2012.
Szwed, John F. Liner notes for *The Magic City*. Evidence 22069-2. 1993.
———. *Space Is The Place: The Lives and Times of Sun Ra*. With a discography by Robert L. Campbell. New York: Pantheon, 1997.
Whitman, Walt. *Leaves of Grass: Comprehensive Reader's Edition*. Eds. Harold W. Blodgett and Sculley Bradley. New York: W. W. Norton & Company, 1968.

Discography is available in Robert L. Campbell's *The Earthly Recordings of Sun Ra* (Cadence Jazz Books, 1994) or in Szwed. John Szwed's scholarly biography is the only book-length study of Sun Ra readily available—a handy compendium of information. So, as in the case of Joni Mitchell, I have had to rely on one book more than scholarly conventions deem advisable. At this point in time, the four major Sun Ra scholars are Robert L. Campbell, John Corbett, Hartmut Geerken and John F. Szwed. They have all been crucial informants for my undertaking.

Appendix: Musical Highlights from The Complete Detroit Jazz Center Residency

Disc 1: A very generous serving of jazz standards. John Gilmore takes a superb tenor solo on "'Round Midnight" (the Thelonious Monk composition). "Cocktails for Two" gets a highly mutated rendition. The Ra original "Love in Outer Space" has a funky organ solo and whistles in the style of a Haitian ra-ra procession. (Perhaps a sonic pun. Ra likes to work his adopted name in whenever he can!) James Jacson's Ancient Egyptian Infinity Drum also gets a long workout on this number's very serious drum break—even longer ones are to follow in this box set!—before the piece's huge, dramatic finish.

Disc 2: The end of the first set on Friday December 26, 1980, showcases a brief and wacky a cappella reading of "Interplanetary Music." The second set has some noteworthy "untitled improv[isations]." Track 9 has a fine John Gilmore tenor solo with some serious skronk (what Arkestra fans refer to when the reed player goes up into pitches only dogs can hear interspersed with low honking—challenging listening at first which was designed to drive off the uncommitted). The next track has some simultaneous soloing in the spirit of the free jazz movement (despite Ra's dislike for it, and even for freedom for that matter!). His last "Unidentified Title," oddly enough, has a kind of Bach feel to it with its sinuous variations on a musical theme. From Szwed's biography, however, it is apparent that Sun Ra was well-versed in the classical canon courtesy of at least Lula Hopkins Randall, a professor from Alabama A & M for Negroes [sic] (*Space* 27).

Disc 3: We open with "Spontaneous Simplicity," a wonderful and understated Ra composition. "Images," which follows, contributes a soaring Michael Ray trumpet solo. The rare "Stompy Jones" is very funky and gut-bucket.

Disc 4: The first Saturday set opens with impressive Marshall Allen skronk. A brief flute interlude is followed by Tony Bethel on trombone, more skronk from Gilmore, a Michael Ray and Walter Miller trumpet duet, and more skronk from Allen: the Arkestra following its director's urgings to play the impossible to provide cosmic tones for mental therapy. Then Ra himself steps in with an intermittently mellow organ solo. Another "Unidentified Title" offers lashings of musical exotica with its percussion effects. And finally with regard to highlights, Sun Ra uses his organ to imitate a subway train arriving and leaving on the bookends of their cover of "Take the A Train."

Disc 5: This is the first disc in the set to show you some virtually unheard, ultra-weird facets of Ra (yes, beyond the high standards already available). It begins with "Slippery Horn," well-played if innocuous kitsch designed perhaps to lull the listener into a false state of relaxation. "Solitude," with its dramatic and showy organ, hints at the turbulence to come. Ra's "Right Road, Wrong Direction" rap from *The Antique Blacks* (see above) evolves into a full-blown, angry diatribe against Planet Earth, "a cursed and doomed planet." It gets even wilder with the "Bad Truth" declamation. Ra screams and shouts: "The truth about the nations of Planet Earth is a BAD truth ... . The history of the people of Planet Earth is a BAD truth." Then Ra turns into a drill sergeant and gets the band and audience marching in a manner reminiscent of his childhood membership in the Boy Scouts knockoff American Woodmen Junior Division (see Szwed 9):

> Shoulder to shoulder
> Man to man
> March as men should
> March as men should

Ra's militancy gets augmented by the band playing a marching beat to this. He exhorts the audience to "fight against the common enemy of all humanity, namely DEEEAAATHHH!": "Don't be a slave / Lay down in the grave / Bow down in the dust." These proceedings are very theatrical. It's almost like hearing a play (cf. his collaboration with Amiri Baraka).

Lastly, he reminds his audience that "When you travel through outer space, you use the password, the word of victory: Ra, Ra, Ra Ra Ra!"

The band turns into his cheerleaders. Even for Ra, this is as weird as it gets. His switch to "Over the Rainbow" on piano chills things out and cools them down. But for a few minutes the listener can hear how ambitious (and, yes, strange) Ra's agenda is: to unite humanity and get them to leave Earth, the planet of death and false freedom (freedom to die), for his discipline and the immortality of outer space travel and living mythology.

Disc 6: Another deluxe version of "Love in Outer Space" occurs, with "alien" groans and guffaws during James Jacson's Infinity Drum solo.

The second Saturday set also finds Ra in an extremely didactic mood, willing to share with an enraptured audience his unusual and complex beliefs. Over the musical strains of "Discipline 27-II," a frequent setting for such ruminations, he reveals that "the sun is a computer that cannot lie ... the big eye ... God's private eye in the sky ... a cosmic spy." The sun sees all, knows all and tells God what's really going on in the solar system, especially on Earth. Ra once again draws a line in the sand between himself and the audience—until they sign up for his space program:

> Everything is my brother except man and woman ... on Planet Earth ... . Am I 666? What kind of mystery am I? ... You're the alien. You have no birth certificates; you have death certificates. So I pronounce you dead until you can prove to me you're alive. Is it right for people to bow to Death? That's your master. The Unknown sent me to break all the laws of nature. I am authorized to do wrong. The universe sent me to be wicked and evil ... . You talk about rights for women ... . Do you have rights for angels? No! ... How do you dare go into outer space? You're just babies in the universe.

There are obvious evocations of all kinds of Gnostic and neoplatonic thought here, all of which Ra voraciously read. The creator of Earth is an inferior deity (the Gnostic demiurge), and what is threatening that creation is paradoxically a higher good—so Satan and Cain can be heroes in this context. Sun Ra always wanted to be, as such, both good and evil to accomplish what he saw as his other-worldly task.

Keeping with the martial theme of the previous set, the "Astro Nation" chant (discussed above in the context of *Live in Cleveland*) gets a tattoo drumbeat accompaniment for the marching Arkestra and audience.

Disc 7: "Lights on a Satellite" features an extended Gilmore solo with Marshall Allen and Danny Ray Thompson on flute backup.

Disc 8: The last part of the second Saturday set has a great and stoic version of the new space chant "Strange Celestial Road": "We're traveling a strange celestial road / to endless ever." The road-weariness of the Arkestra really comes through. As it should, for these two shows (on discs 4-8) pushed the band about as far as it could go!

Disc 9: After the *sturm und drang* of the night before, the Sunday matinee begins on a suitably restrained note with Marshall Allen plucking the *kora* (a traditional African stringed instrument). This use of an ancient musical platform is reminiscent of the slogan of Chicago's AACM movement (the Associated Artists of Creative Music): "ancient to the future." These musicians, including Muhal Richard Abrams and members of the Art Ensemble of Chicago heard Ra and were influenced by him (Szwed 176). Some would even play with him in Europe as members of the 1983 Sun Ra All Stars.

John Gilmore mellows the crowd even more with a be-bop cover of "Jingle Bells" in honor of the season. "Hymn to the Sun" is a gentle composition for flutes that seamlessly leads into the invocation and arrival of the man himself, "the living myth." As Ra often did, he tells the audience "You can call me Mister Mystery." This time he lives up to his name by introducing brand new material the compilers of this box set cannot identify even to this day. Track 3 contains a wild baritone sax solo from Danny Ray Thompson with lots of choogling and backing from trumpet and French horn. This piece is followed by a very angular composition for bassoon, flute, trumpet and French horn with no percussion until the very end of the piece—real outer space music! Track 4 is an odd, very deliberative original for organ. The band's eventual entrance into the piece and subsequent repetitive playing of the main motif lead me to believe this is an unknown number of the "Discipline" series of Ra compositions.

Disc 10: Here we have a rare live "Sleeping Beauty" with Ra singing in a relaxed mood backed by on-point vocal harmonies—which also grace the following "Fate in a Pleasant Mood." Ra assures us "The time is fast approaching when fate will be in a pleasant mood." This mood arrives with the Ra classic "El is a Sound of Joy," which has a jumping middle section and Michael Ray cutting loose in addition to the basic presentation. "South America" is a Latin-influenced number with a massive percussion line. Ra and the band continue the positivity with the wistful vocals:

> South America, such a nice place ... .
> I plan to visit there one day.

Appendix: Detroit Jazz Center Discs

> And if it's as nice as they say it is,
> Perhaps I'll be tempted to stay ... .
> I know I'm going to stay.
> Ole!

The geographical tour continues with "Africa," which we are assured is a "romantic land of treasure ... . There's never skies so blue as in Africa." The percussionists drive the beat hard and stretch it out, eventuating in another Infinity Drum solo. These works showcase not only Ra's more earthbound side (and after the day before, certainly more Earth-friendly approach!) as well as his interest in lounge music and exotica. (Les Baxter could have readily covered this material.) The matinee ends with space chants about Ra's very favorite place, Saturn, his home planet: "Saturn rings, rings around Saturn ... . Who put those rings around Saturn? ... I am Sun Ra, Lord of the Saturn Rings." (Eat your heart out, Sauron!)

Disc 11: The evening show on Sunday finds Ra returning to a tutorial mood, revisiting his more esoteric doctrines (again to the tune of "Discipline 27-II"): "Time was crucified 2,000 years ago ... . You are living on the other side of time ... . Confusion and chaos knock on every door ... . I have come to make you confess to me 'I know I don't know.'" What he means by this is certainly up for grabs, but I am reminded of science fiction author Philip K. Dick's theory, based on some of his mystical visions, that we are really still living in the first century of the Christian era and the devil is deceiving us to delay the Second Coming. Sun Ra could have encountered these theories in his voracious reading of speculative fiction and would have found them congenial to his basically Gnostic outlook (matter is evil and must be transcended through knowledge, spirit and discipline).

Ra's Sunday anti-sermon also reprises his interest in his demonic side (cf. the night before): "I am the mystery of iniquity ... . I am Sin ... . I bring you pleasure without measure ... the sin that does not bring death ... . In ancient days they knew me ... . It is written ... in the last days Ra will visit the western lands." Compared to this, the Rolling Stones' "Sympathy for the Devil" looks fairly elementary. Here Ra claims to be a conflation of the devil (broadly considered) and the Egyptian god of the sun he takes the name of.

Then we get another blast of solar paranoia: "You've got to mind what you're talking about ... . You've got to give account in judgment ... . The witness against you is the Big Eye in the Sky." John Gilmore gives us the benediction with a hearty dose of tenor skronk, burning the message in our brains with his high-pitched squeals.

Disc 12: Sun Ra calms things down with some jazz standards. As promised in the rare editorial note in the Transparency box set, there is a "[b]eautiful Gilmore solo at [the] end" of "Body and Soul." Marshall Allen also gives a fine closing solo for Coleman Hawkins' "Queer Notions" (a standard the Fletcher Henderson orchestra played when Ra was a member). We are also treated to a rollicking "Discipline 99," highlighted by some fine bass playing from Richard Williams.

Disc 14: The Monday set opens with a nice reading of the "Pleiades" composition for flute and bells. Michael Ray executes some tough circular breathing during an improvisation, which is followed by Gilmore displaying some "sheets of sound" on his saxophone in the idiom of John Coltrane—whom his playing is always in dialogue with but never imitating—as well as some characteristic skronk moves.

Disc 15: The concert continues with an exquisite reading of "Lights on a Satellite" with great solo contributions from both Ra on organ and Gilmore. Ra also shines on "Love in Outer Space," which is also enhanced by the usual great drumming—but in this rendition also by some funky horn riffs for further punctuation. In the initial section of this long performance, there is a more equal distribution of labor among the entire Arkestra than is typical for this song (which is usually an excuse for most of the band to take a bathroom break by all accounts!). Eventually we do get the drummers carrying the burden, the Infinity Drum solo, and a theatrical bit with alien groaning while a band member asks "What planet is this?" (The answer he receives: "Planet Earth.") Then the music gets even quieter as the band plays with "little instruments" (to use the stock phrase from Art Ensemble of Chicago albums—the group which pioneered these ultra-pianissimo effects for the new jazz in the late sixties). A soaring full-band Cadillac arrangement of the main theme brings this epic version of the piece to a climax. The follow-up "We'll Be Together Again" also swings with just organ and drums, building up to a dramatic solo conclusion on the former instrument.

Disc 16: After all this fine playing, Sun Ra felt that some discourse was in order. He announces that "the spaceship Earth is scheduled to be leaving soon ... to find another place in the sun" because it is "at present living in the shadow of death"—as opposed to "the shadow of other planets" which are "converging" on Earth. Ra laments that he "could've enjoyed [him]self on this planet if the people had been alive." But they're not, so it's time to go! A series of typical space chants follow. The band encores with another martial march version of "Astro Nation," a sparkling Gilmore solo on "King Porter Stomp,"

Appendix: Detroit Jazz Center Discs

and a stately version of "Fate in a Pleasant Mood." On this last, the organ performs the vocal line to good effect and solos a little; the a cappella vocals, briefly accompanied by a little sax, get softer and softer to end the show.

Disc 17: The Tuesday show opens with some good skronk from Gilmore in the improvisation that leads into "Discipline 27." Marshall Allen also gives us some skronk showmanship on his alto saxophone to set the mood for Ra's apocalyptic warning: "Impressions misinterpreted can destroy a planet." Whimsy is mixed in with the warnings this time: "People walk around in a daze ... . The daze makes them crazy ... . They're crazy as a daisy." Then we get some standards, including a very upbeat and up-tempo "What's New?" (pretty consistently the way Ra likes to cover it in contrast with the more wistful and dolorous reading given the piece by the likes of, for example, Linda Ronstadt).

Disc 18: Amidst the standards, Ra sneaks in his classic composition "Lights on a Satellite"—lovely and subdued with lots of Gilmore soloing. Another editorial note for "Love in Outer Space": "40 minutes!" Yep. This is the most epic reading of the piece available, full of the Arkestra's complete bag of tricks: hocketing and staccato playing by the reeds and horns, percussive banging on metal sheets to give an industrial sound, the "What planet is this?" skit, little instruments, a long Infinity Drum solo. The "Enlightenment" vocal invitation to "be of our space world" is reinforced by an extra-raucous opening of "The Shadow World" from both the reeds and horns and Ra on exuberant organ and synthesizer.

Disc 19: "The Shadow World" continues with some serious Marshall Allen skronk at very high pitches, preceding the already available "Journey to Stars Beyond" discussed above. After that sublime strangeness, "Over the Rainbow" settles things down (as it did on disk five after the "Shoulder to Shoulder" → "Ra Ra Ra" sequence). It's Ra's way of acknowledging that we're not in Kansas (or Detroit) anymore! "Space Is the Place" has gut-bucket tenor and baritone sax soloing that at one point even quotes from "Tequila"! The chants offer a slight lyrical variant on "Moonship Journey": "*Prepare yourself for the* moonship journey" (my italics).

Disc 20: These last nine discs capture the excitement of the three culminating concerts on New Year's Eve of 1980. The eight o'clock set begins with a long improvisation with the African *kora*, percussion, and the horns intermittently probing like sonar signals (cf. "Atlantis"). A beautiful untitled flute composition follows, very much in the spirit of Ra's "Pleiades" pieces. The music gets gradually edgier and more akin to free jazz, culminating in an overlay of "Auld Lang Syne" over the mounting cacophony of the simultaneous soloing. June Tyson's "Astro Black" vocal is accompanied by nice trumpet flourishes from Michael Ray. A rare performance of "Tapestry from an Asteroid" ensues: a Tyson showcase about the "space joy" you receive when you get "vibrations from an asteroid" (then "the spaceways are not so far"). And finally the standard processional "Along Came Ra." We are reminded that there was a time, pre-Ra, "when the world was in darkness / and darkness was ignorance." Thanks to Ra, now darkness is "Astro Black," not ignorance. After over half an hour of gorgeous music, Sun Ra steps on stage.

He begins by conducting "Discipline 27" with lots of dramatic interludes from various instruments between statements of the main theme, thereby showcasing the band. Michael Ray contributes much wildness and more sonic sonar probing; seasonal sleigh bells and other percussion frolic (including what the Art Ensemble of Chicago call "little instruments"); more horns crescendo. Then we get a mellow change of pace with a rare reading of "Island in the Sun," an organ-and-percussion-based idyll augmented with horns and flute that provides a smooth transition to the standards to follow.

Disc 21: The Gershwin brothers' "A Foggy Day" begins with that heavy Ra ballpark organ before easing into a jaunty full-band chart with deft solos. A sultry "How Am I to Know?" follows with fine solos from alto sax Marshall Allen and (again) trumpeter Michael Ray. Ra sneaks in a few of his own compositions bidding for the jazz canon, including a swinging "Images" with a lyrical tenor solo from John Gilmore that evolves into an organ duet with Ra. "There Will Never Be Another You" showcases more tenor splendor from Gilmore, followed by the meditative Ra / Ray dialogue "Celestial Realms" already discussed in its El Saturn appearance on *Oblique Parallax* above. A fine reading of the ubiquitous "Enlightenment" sets us up for the intense sermonizing about to follow.

Disc 22: From this extended residency, we can observe something pertinent about Sun Ra as a teacher—and indeed he always regarded pedagogy as a major aspect of his mission on Earth. I only saw him twice at one-night stands (D.C. Space in Washington, Glam Slam in Minneapolis). Both times he downplayed the sermonizing in favor of standards, original compositions and space chants. Ra had to have a special relationship with an audience—the weekly gigs at Slug's in New York, his annual appearance at the Ann Arbor Jazz and Blues Fes-

Appendix: Detroit Jazz Center Discs

tival for a while, or a residency like this—to carry the lessons further. As we saw already on disc five, he felt unusually comfortable conveying his belief system to this audience. (One suspects, for starters, there were a number of repeaters who would attend multiple shows.) In any case, here on New Year's Eve he really lets it rip.

After a lovely (and rare) vocal duet with June Tyson on "Somebody Else's World," he unveils his quasi-Gnostic opinion that this world was NOT his idea; in fact, it's "a damnable conception": "in my most evilest moments, I wouldn't make a world like this" (throughout, all this is accompanied by hypnotic drumming akin to a voodoo ceremony). He practically screams at the audience in his passionate declamation that "this planet is a disgrace to the devil and a shame to God. This planet is out of order." Only "the unknown ... magic myths of the impossible" can save his auditors from the pain of this existence. He puts a specific historical spin on his jeremiad by reminding us "somebody might push the button" (a reference to the re-heating of the Cold War in 1980 and a dry run for his later "Nuclear War") and asserting that "the truth about the President on Planet Earth is a bad truth" (a nod to the arrival of Ronald Reagan).

After the nuclear fire and brimstone, he makes his cryptic altar (alter?) call: "The impossible is your only hope ... . Join my mythocracy." When I give talks about Sun Ra, audiences always wonder what this would entail—as well they might. It's clearly reminiscent of what existentialist philosopher Soren Kierkegaard called "the leap of faith." As was the case with his leap to faith in a mysterious God, the leap to Ra's mythocracy is "impossible" and absurd. You have to believe ridiculous stuff ultimately (e.g., that Sun Ra is from Saturn). But I believe he was serious about this, not a pure con man. As with the Masons, there were / are degrees of initiation ranging from actually joining the Arkestra to being a casual fan who likes the music without getting into all the weird stuff. As with any other belief system, levels of commitment and engagement will vary. And Sun Ra completely understood this. But like Sly Stone, he wanted to take us higher in a great black tradition that goes back to tribal priests through Marcus Garvey to not just Sun Ra, but the shamanistic grooves of James Brown.

June Tyson adds to the consummate strangeness at this point by doing vocalese that sounds like a moog synthesizer. A few more imprecations hurled at Planet Earth ensue: "What has Planet Earth done for you? Even the first man and woman ended up bad." Then the band breaks out in a fierce improvisation redolent with skronking reeds and repeated crescendos—an unleashing of all the pent-up emotion

Ra's sermon has inspired and a translation of its message into musical sound. Finally, some calm resumes as the Arkestra pulls back to just acoustic bass, percussion and drums and trumpet. Sun Ra and June Tyson share vocals again on "They'll Come Back," which in turn inspires Ra to reveal a few more truths from the magic myth world: "Prepare to meet them … . Other worlds wish to speak to you through the universal language: music. I know they exist because they sent me to you."

Brilliantly, Sun Ra re-conceptualizes the leap of faith as a gamble (in terms reminiscent of the chess game battle with the devil in the film *Space Is the Place*): "I took a big gamble on you. Take the big gamble on me. Take the big gamble on the dark horse … . It's a fixed race. If I win, I win. If I lose, I win. I'm the dark horse." Perhaps he's getting at his own sense of cosmic connection beyond the beleaguered fate of 1980's Earth. He's part of the universe, not just tied to Earth. We need him; he doesn't necessarily need us.

End of the set, except for him interrupting the emcee with his special offer to the audience: "You are cordially invited to visit Planet Saturn any time you choose. Any time you want to visit Planet Saturn, get your passport from me."

Disc 23: After the usual improvisational warm-up, the eleven o'clock set begins in earnest with a closely harmonized a cappella "When There Is No Sun." Sun Ra continues his heavily theatrical performance from the last set with a zany query to the audience: "Are you spotless? I am the sun. I have spots. Sun spots. Just because I have spots, does that make me sin? Well then, I'm sin. I'm still the sun." One can only speculate where Ra learned of this imagery, so redolent of my Catholic religious training regarding sin as stains on the soul.

After this setup, "Discipline 27- II" kicks in, where Ra reveals more over the vamp: "I am the Tempter. I've come to tempt you to leave Planet Earth, This is a cursed place … . I'm the troubleshooter of the universe. I never visit a planet until there is no hope. I do not belong to any particular one planet. I use planets for stepping stones." This commodious composition takes the concert right up to the New Year and a swinging (and straight-up) "Auld Lang Syne"—Sun Ra channeling Guy Lombardo just because he can! (Admittedly, a brief interpolation of "Pop Goes the Weasel" mutates the moment a bit.)

Then the Arkestra morph into a full-blown, blast-from-the-past old time dancehall big band with a deluxe poker face cover of "Big John's Special" replete with lovely tenor soloing from John Gilmore. Ra's own composition "El Is the Sound of Joy" gets a similar reverential

Appendix: Detroit Jazz Center Discs

pastiche. After the electronic explorations of "Beyond the Purple Star Zone" (available elsewhere as noted), the band plays the lesser-known piece called "The World of Africa": an epic tsunami of polyrhythmic percussion so hypnotically trance-inducing that it makes up for what it lacks in complex melody through its therapeutic value. (Not for nothing did Sun Ra title one of his releases *Cosmic Tones for Mental Therapy*.) After that frenzied workout, the standard "Rose Room" gets us back in a mellow lounge mood with Gilmore and Ray kicking it very old school in their gentle solos.

Disc 24: This CD opens with an ultra-rare vocal version of "Halloween in Harlem." For some reason, this composition has become one of my all-time favorite pieces by Sun Ra. Perhaps it's because of its loping melodic complexity which reminds us that Ra was right up there as a composer with the two American guys named Charles (Ives and Mingus). Or maybe it's the thematic riffing on white fears—for the bulk of Ra's listening audience was always ofay. (He was and is too strange for many African Americans.) What could be more super-spooky than to spend Halloween in Harlem? Never mind that this was performed on a completely different holiday: he is Mr. Mystery. The deep voice of bassist Richard Williams ups the uncanniness of it all.

The band takes us even farther out, off-planet, on a "Journey to Saturn" with Ra's usual offering of one-way or round-trip tickets. His exhortations to leave Earth end up in a recitation of "Never Never Land" from *Peter Pan*, an early indication of his interest in Walt Disney.

This disc also showcases an extremely rare bop vocal version of "Medicine for a Nightmare," the nightmare in question being—you guessed it—life on Earth: "You need this medicine bad!" Following this, Marshall Allen provides some strong alto medicine with a skronking solo of alien animal cries so high-pitched that it actually cleans out my sinuses when I listen to it. That's real medicine! A very dramatic reading of "Rocket Number Nine" led by John Gilmore follows while Ra informs us that "the Space Age is here to stay" over the "Zoom! Zoom! Up in the air!" backdrop. He explains that "the music of the Space Age" is "not mind music, it's music of the unknown ... . Even if you don't understand, you still got to face the music." An appropriate setting for the a cappella soulful vocal harmonizing on "Face the Music" which follows.

Disc 25: The music to be faced turns out to be W.C. Handy's "St. Louis Blues," a song Ra has also recorded on solo piano. Here it gets the royal treatment with majestic solos from Gilmore and Ray, a fine walking bass line from Richard Williams and a Ra vocal. I can see why he'd connect with the song; it's about departure, even if it's only about leaving the Gateway to the West and not Earth: "If I feel tomorrow like I do today / I'm going to pack my trunk and make my getaway."

The more terrestrial groundedness continues for the next three songs, beginning with an organ-heavy "Watusi" with rare Ra scat vocalizing before the standard "What planet is this?" theatrics and an Infinity Drum solo from James Jacson. June Tyson sings of the "Lion of the Heavens," the sun. Then we get another of my all-time favorites, "Planet Earth," with vocal harmonizing from Tyson, Ra and Gilmore before the band marches around the venue: "This song an anthem is of Planet Three, Planet Earth." Ensuing space chants remind us that Earth is only "the third heaven." We can "try Pluto too," or anywhere our imagination takes us: "If we come from nowhere here, why can't we go somewhere there?"

Disc 26: The last three o'clock in the morning set cuts right to the chase with a straight-ahead rendition of the standard "On Green Dolphin Street" featuring a solid contribution from John Gilmore's tenor sax. After this, Michael Ray performs a be-bop trumpet improvisation interacting with the drum line and the reed section. June Tyson takes us back to the cosmos with her sung assurance that "outer space is such a pleasant place." Then Sun Ra gives a far more succinct declamation: "if you're not a myth, whose reality are you? If you're not a reality, whose myth are you?" A puzzling dualism for the uninitiated (or even the partially initiated). He's a poet, not a philosopher.

Disc 27: An untitled group improvisation—heavy on saxes, drums and trumpet—woke up the sleepers. The wildness continued with "Vista Omniverse" for organ and synthesizer, which inspires one auditor (band or audience member?) to interject "right on, man, right on" and "mmmm." Then we get audio whiplash from a bevy of big-band standards, an appropriate move given the lateness of the hour. Sun Ra has done enough preaching for the night. Highlights include a "Tea for Two" which segues from a shimmering organ solo to full band solos in turn. A rollicking "King Porter Stomp" offers more sonic time travel to the heyday of the big bands. Ra sneaks in a few of his own compositions: the lovely "Interstellar Low Ways" with organ and trumpet showcases, and a martial-beat rendition of "The Satellites Are Spinning." The ultimate standard "Stompin' at the Savoy" keeps up the nostalgic groove, followed by a baritone sax and percus-

Appendix: Detroit Jazz Center Discs

sion driven processional: the Ra original "Mayan Temples." Marshall Allen also works in some nice filigree on flute here.

Disc 28: This last recording from the residency opens with an unidentified title, possibly a rare number of his "Discipline" series. Like the others, it is fairly repetitious—but in a good way. The track has a nice feel of carnival parade to it. Coleman Hawkins' be-bop classic "Queer Notions" succeeds, then a soulful organ workout on "Willow Weep for Me." As per his practice, Ra inserts another older original (the bopping "Space Loneliness") amongst the standards—and indeed Thelonious Monk's "'Round Midnight" comes next, distinguished by good solos from Ra on organ and the reed section, culminating in sheets of sound off Marshall Allen's alto to close the piece. A suitably *echt* "Limehouse Blues" gives us the frenzied feel of a Tex Avery cartoon before the Arkestra slows down for a stately "Discipline 99." The concert closes with standard fare: "Space Is the Place" (with a noisy synthesizer burst) and some space chants. Like many others, Ra gets his math slightly wrong when he reminds the audience it's "only nineteen years" until the twenty-first century ("The year 2000 is knocking at your door"). In any case, the Omniverse Jet Set Arkestra was, and is, ready, willing and able to hug that future.

Afterword: What's New?

Since I wrote all these words about Sun Ra, a fair amount of activity has continued to occur which makes more and more of his body of work accessible in varying degrees. I am going to concentrate my attention on the newly available music (CDs, streaming services and YouTube respectively) with a further glance at visual documents and writing concerning Ra – both by him and about him. Unlike my book chapter, I will be extremely selective and brief in my coverage, providing just enough information for the intrigued to be able to pursue their own explorations.

Unquestionably the biggest development since my previous writing is the 2011 box set *Sun Ra: The Eternal Myth Revealed, Volume I*. This fourteen CD compilation curated by former Arkestra member and Sun Ra Music Archive Executive Director Michael Anderson covers, rather exhaustively, rare material from 1914-1959 (Sun Ra's arrival on Earth up until the eve of his departure from Chicago). Several ironies are in play here. The close reader will recall that Anderson disparaged Transparency, the label that distributed this set, as a purveyor of bootlegs. Clearly, Transparency's founder Michael Sheppard and Anderson had a rapprochement that enabled this release to occur. Secondly, the box set promises a forthcoming second volume covering 1960-1980. Eight years later, this release has not appeared. And since Transparency's head passed away in 2016, it will presumably not be coming out – at least not on this particular label.

What we do have is exhaustive documentation of Sun Ra's earliest music, including avant-garde experiments on church organs and electronic instruments, recordings made on paper (rather than magnetic) tape recorders, and much in the way of interspersed commentary by Michael Anderson and Ra himself in interview. The provenance of some of this material is less than definitive: a comment made by Ra that discusses working with a particular musician on more than one occasion leads to a speculative inclusion of a track that ostensibly sounds like Ra could have played on it or arranged it. The listener does not always hear what Anderson notices. Nonetheless, the majority of this material is indisputably a result of Sun Ra's involvement in varying degrees. The other major exception would be the presence herein of recordings by musicians who influenced Sun Ra, such as the pianist Mary Lou Williams, included to give additional context to his sonic origins.

The nearly seventeen hours of sound is certainly more than the sum of its parts. The major revelation a listener gets from this archival journey is that Sun Ra, despite his interest in outer space, was not working in a vacuum (ouch). As in the case of Frank Zappa's fusion of Viennese school classical music and gutbucket rhythm and blues, Sun Ra demonstrates that one can achieve utter originality by simply combining disparate musics. As the incomparable jazz pianist Cecil Taylor observed in the liner notes to his 1990 release *In Florescence*, "[e]veryone has their own way of organizing sound." Sun Ra's approach was to absorb thoroughly every single aspect of African American popular music (spirituals, blues, jazz in all its garden varieties and permutations, soulful crooners, streetcorner doo wop, folkish novelties like patting juba [body slapping for percussion]) and then meld those vast resources to the soundscapes of musical exotica, nascent electronic music and the themes of science fiction and Ra's own esoteric metaphysical interests discussed above. The results are utterly unique, but Michael Anderson's collection helps you see all the strands of interest: a clarification nonetheless incapable of demystifying Mister Mystery!

Probably my favorite discovery in this musical trove was a full documentation of Sun Ra's arrangements for the Hambone Kids with the Red Saunders Orchestra on "Hambone," "Zekiel, Zekiel" and "Piece of Puddin'" (disc 6). These novelty items, as well as his vocal coaching of Sugar Chile Robinson on "Bouncin' Ball Boogie" and "I'll Eat My Spinach" (disc 4) confirm that Sun Ra never really lost touch with his inner child. His later novelty Batman material and the Disney covers would lead one to suspect same, but here is early proof positive – and the music is delightful! I would also single out Sun Ra's funny yet plaintive self-analysis on the spoken word poem "If They Only Knew" (disc 3) where he describes himself as God's biggest "joke" perpetrated on an unsuspecting human race. One of Michael Anderson's — and Paul Youngquist's, for that matter — corrective moves in updating our perceptions of Sun Ra's project is to pay greater attention to his words as well as his music. The cosmic alienation of this selection validates the importance of such an approach.

But the real gift of *The Eternal Myth Revealed, Volume I* is to resurrect African American culture in the early half of the previous century in all its rich diversity. This collection would have a value comparable to Harry Smith's *Anthology of American Folk Music* or the releases from Dust-to-Digital records even if Sun Ra was absent as the magnet organizing the cultural filings. His unifying presence, of course, proves far more than a mere bonus, although unquestionably Ra's finest work came later than the 1959 cut-off date for Anderson's collection.

Such a consideration brings us to the next most important Sun Ra recent posthumous release, a lost album entitled *Thunder of the Gods* released by Modern Harmonic, the latest label to provide new Sun Ra material. Half of the record is a live version of "Calling Planet Earth" dating from the early 1970s, mainly distinguished by fortuitous microphone placement at opposing sides of the stage to give an unusually cinematic glimpse of the soloists in motion as they pace the venue. The other two tracks ("Moonshots Across the Sky" and "Thunder of the Gods") offer the more revelatory listening. As Christopher Eddy's liner notes indicate, these tracks come from the fallout of Sun Ra's May 1966 college tour of New York state campuses, when the band bought various instruments that they did not know how to play. Sun Ra's experimental "study in ignorance" led to the *Strange Strings* release; nearly a half century later, we have the sequel.

I will resist the urge to provide any kind of listening guide for the nineteen minutes of auditory throwdown these two tracks offer. Many listeners would simply respond: NOISE! (The sonic equivalent of "my five year old could paint that" legendarily overheard in an art museum in front of an abstract expressionist canvas.) Like that hypothetical painting, this music is abstract. Its only connection with jazz is that it is of course improvised; you will not hear any discernible relation to the blues, however. Domestic animals will become agitated when it is played, anecdotal evidence suggests. Its pleasures ultimately reside from the certainty that it takes you somewhere no other music has if you listen with open ears. One does not hear chaos, or naive banging, but gifted tone scientists, removed from their comfort zone by their leader, attempting the impossible and showing us through sound the landscape of utterly alien worlds and ineffable visions of the entities that inhabit them. On a technical note, the squeaking door featured on the bonus track of *Strange Strings* pops up again here as a musical accent on "Thunder of the Gods" accompanying the strings and percussion.

On a slightly less challenging level, Cosmic Myth Records (another new purveyor of Ra material) has reissued a remastered and expanded edition of *My Brother the Wind, Volume 1*. This 1970 release, recorded in 1969, was Sun Ra's celebration of the improvisatory capacities of Moog synthesizers, his entry into the solar system of Walter / Wendy Carlos, Tomita, Beaver and Krause, and Perry and Kingsley. Other than improved sound quality, this CD offers a larger selection of Ra electronica: a repurposed "Space Probe" from other El Saturn releases and the single release "The Perfect Man," here included with all the alternate takes and false starts that show Sun Ra's rapid learning curve on these new keyboards.

What impresses the open ear is how rapidly Ra made the Moog his very own tool for sonic exploration. No one ever played it like him before or since; he used it as a sonic canvas for his extraterrestrial mind travels. Only the composer Edgard Varese craved and needed the resources of electronic instruments as much as Sun Ra did (check out Varese's "Deserts" and "Poeme Electronique"). Like Varese, Ra knew exactly how he could use these devices to realize his platonic ideas. And as in the case of *Thunder of the Gods*, one would have to stretch one's definitions of jazz to the breaking point to file this release in that genre! But of course, one needn't: it's just music when all is said and done.

Another Modern Harmonic release worth noting briefly is *Exotica*. As its title suggests, this two disc compilation tries to bring together all of Ra's work that resembles the space age bachelor pad atmospherics of Les Baxter, Martin Denny and Esquivel. As such, the collection makes a valid critical point as well as providing pre-ambient background listening pleasures. Most of the material is culled from existing Sun Ra releases, but there are a few nuggets to interest the completist: an unedited full version of "Island in the Sun" and some unreleased rarities ("April in Paris" and the Ra jewel "Cha-Cha in Outer Space" [!]). Of course Sun Ra could cha-cha.... The CD features great cover art from space landscapist Chesley Bonestell as well.

My next stop on this highly truncated tour is the one archival live concert release worth a mention, *The Sun Ra Arkestra Live in Nickelsdorf 1984*. As with all the recent live releases I'm not discussing, there isn't anything here I haven't previously alluded to in the Ra canon. I like this concert because it's fairly complete (three disks) and a good sampling of what the band was performing in that era (including "Nuclear War" and "East of the Sun"). The peculiar racist vibes of European releases recurs in this German import: why are there monkeys featured on the cover art? The liner notes by Hans Falb are much more respectful, comparing Ra to James Joyce and Arno Schmidt (author of the mammoth experimental tome *Zettel's Traum* [*Bottom's Dream*]). Overall, the packaging is paradoxical at best.

And finally with regard to CDs, I must recommend a comparatively new release (2015) from the ghost band "under the direction of Marshall Allen" from the Babylon Club in Istanbul in 2014 (*Babylon*). This concert thoughtfully includes a longer DVD version of the show so the uninitiated can see the concert spectacle. There are a few unreleased Ra compositions as well as live rarities such as "Unmask the Batman" and a closing "Hit That Jive Jack" space chant. The Arkestra itself contains a hybrid of younger apprentice players, including the highly serviceable Farid Barron holding down Ra's keyboard spot, and venerable veterans such as Marshall Allen himself. Long may they live and prosper!

CDs and vinyl are now very much retro ways to access this music (still much beloved by older fans like myself as well as vinyl fetishists). Streaming platforms such as Spotify and MP3 files are far more common listening options. There is a certain complementarity at work: music that one can stream may not be available as a disk or record at any given moment – and vice versa. For example, at the moment of this writing the Sun Ra collection *Exotica* described above is not available on a streaming service (vs. other Modern Harmonic titles such as *Thunder of the Gods*) but it is available on vinyl, CD or as an MP3 download.

What I want to address here are some recent releases on these streaming services that are not readily available on compact disk (at the moment, subject to ready change). I would first cite two recent (2019) solo keyboard compilations: *Solo Piano at WKCR 1977* and *Solo Keyboard Minnesota 1978*. The former piano recital originates from a show on the Columbia University campus station and features wonderful if typical readings of covers associated with this type of Ra performance at the time: "St. Louis Blues," "Sophisticated Lady," "Take the 'A' Train." As always, I sense an extra level of involvement in "Tryin to Put the Blame on Me" (an original or an obscure cover?): as with the later "Down Here on the Ground," Sun Ra's identification with the lyrics give the song an interesting edge ("If I'm the cause of it all / That makes me the boss"). Regrettably, the vocal is intially mixed rather low on this recording until it is adjusted.

The 1978 Minnesota outing alternates between piano and the Crumar Mainman synthesizer Sun Ra was favoring at the time (cf. *Disco 3000*). On this release one gets to hear not only originals such as "Cosmo-Surrepetitious" and "Discipline Precision" on the beast (providing an interesting sonic comparison with the Moog solos on *My Brother the Wind, Volume 1*), but a striking cover of the sorrow song "Sometimes I Feel Like a Motherless Child" on the synth, a reading which manages to be both very emotional and oblique at the same time — perhaps because Ra is signifying in part about his alien origins?

Then there is *Universe in Blue* (2014). This was originally a 1972 El Saturn release by "Sun Ra and His Blue Universe Arkestra" so obscure that it does not grace the discography in the back of John Szwed's biography. The song titles emphasize the colors black and blue (e.g., "When the Black Man Ruled This Land," "In a Blue Mood"). The mood overall is reflective and meditative, featuring Sun Ra on restrained organ, another facet of the diamond especially suited for listening in the wee hours.

The Invisible Shield (2014) is another El Saturn release (this time from 1974) that slipped through the cracks of the initial Szwed / Campbell discography in *Space Is the Place*. An interesting mix of standards and originals, the streaming version has a bonus track cover of Gershwin's "But Not for Me" (see below for more George Gershwin from Sun Ra!). *Peace on Earth* (2011) was a posthumous release from the London- based jazz label Wnts

[sic]. The provenance of this collection is a bit sketchy as a result (dates? locations?), but there are a few jokers in the deck alongside of the usual suspects ("Round Midnight," "Planet Earth," "Enlightenment") that make this worth the phone touch: a reading of the lovely standard "You Never Told Me That You Care" and the cha-cha "Great Balls of Fire" (no discernible relation to Jerry Lee Lewis I can detect). Wherever this is coming from, it's definitely legitimate Ra.

And finally, I must mention the collection available for streaming entitled *Sun Ra Plays Gershwin* (2017). As in the case of *Exotica* or some of the doo wop vocal group anthologies, this assemblage is designed to make a critical point: over his long career, Sun Ra covered enough Gershwin material to fill an album. Unlike his Disney covers, however, this material was never showcased particularly by a touring ensemble. Rather it was interspersed in set lists and album releases over the years, obviously adding up.

The opening "Rhapsody in Blue" is the only completely unreleased item here (as opposed to an early alternate take of " 'S Wonderful" with Hattie Randolph), a stately yet mutated reading of Gershwin's magnum opus along reliable Arkestra lines. A second version of " 'S Wonderful" by the Arkestra is nice and jaunty. Some of the versions of Gershwin here are from the Nu Sounds doo wop Ra productions ("Nice Work if You Can Get It," "A Foggy Day"). John Gilmore takes soulfully mellow solos on "It Ain't Necessarily So" and "I Loves You Porgy." "But Not for Me" features intricate piano and great trumpet work (Michael Ray?); "The Man I Love" has Sun Ra playing a solovox like vibes and violin with Wilbur Ware on guitar (probably from the early 1950s).

Overall, this is a worthwhile project for its convenience, primarily; I'm not sure this would convert a Gershwin aficionado to Ra's music. But who knows? It certainly provides fuel for refuting any remaining skeptics who might doubt Ra's musical abilities on the basis of his more experimental sonic forays by offering evidence they would have to acknowledge as legitimate.

But for some of us it can't get too edgy and far out! Which brings me to the uses of Sun Ra on YouTube. Often it may be the case that a release not available on other platforms will be gifted to the world via a YouTube video. Most spectacularly, this is the case for a portion of the Holy Grail of Sun Ra collectors: the last two releases on El Saturn, *Hidden Fire 1* and *2*. All 39'46" of the first volume documenting these 1988 shows at the Knitting Factory in New York is available gratis on YouTube. Since "My Brothers The Wind and Sun #9", half of volume 2, is a bonus track on Leo's live release *A Night in East Berlin* (available in diverse formats), only two unidentified titles from the second vinyl are unavailable to the curious listener — unless they're willing to fork over $560.67 to the two German collectors currently selling copies of the album on <discogs.com>!

I love the 75% of this January 29, 1988 concert I have been able to hear, and suspect that for the vast majority of planet Earth 0% would readily suffice. El Saturn shut its doors as a purveyor of vinyl on the strongest possible note: as Szwed has rhapsodized, this is utterly uncompromising late Ra, one last cosmic explosion before a somewhat mellower old age.

I am reluctant to provide much in the way of program notes here as well. There are no recognizable melodies; the synthesizer is set as gritty as it can go; Art Jenkins vibrates his lips and screams space vocals like an extraterrestrial blues shouter into a metal megaphone. Domestic animals in earshot tremble; sinuses clear; outer space is definitely in the house. Have a listen and see where it takes YOU! The Arkestra's stars were in a most unusual alignment that evening, perhaps because of Art Jenkins' guest appearance authorizing the impossible.

With the death of Michael Sheppard and the Transparency label, the video output of Sun Ra's legacy has become more of a trickle, not withstanding the Istanbul Arkestra concert noted above. One fabulous exception, however, was the release of a 40th Anniversary Edition version of Sun Ra's film *Space Is the Place* in 2014 by Harte Recordings of San Francisco. This package has all the bells and whistles anyone could desire: a DVD with two versions of the film (the longer director's cut with twenty minutes of softcore and blaxploitation gestures and the version Sun Ra himself approved for release [hitherto the only version one could see]), a commentary on the former variant of the film by the original producer of it (Jim Newman), a CD with a few bonus tracks that never made it onto the original soundtrack release, and a book with over 100 pages of production stills from the film shoot. The print has been cleaned up for maximal picture quality.

Not only does this presentation supercede all earlier offerings of the film (the video release on Evidence or YouTube giveaways), it forces a needed reevaluation of the work both in terms of the Sun Ra canon (capturing a moment of heightened cultural interest for Ra's activity) and the study of the blaxploitation film genre. Blaxploitation has deservedly received the attention of film scholars as much as other tried and true subcategories as film noir and Italian neorealism, despite the implicit criticism in the label given the genre. The importance of *Space Is the Place* is that it is the only example of a genre fusion of science fiction and blaxploitation. There were a few blaxploitation horror films (*Blacula*, *Blackenstein*, zombie films such as *Sugar Hill* [1974 — not to be confused with the Wesley Snipes 1994 film of the same title]), but most examples of the genre favored action and comedy (in that order).

It strikes the contemporary viewer as slightly odd that this film did not get any love at the box office, given the critical and even commercial success (relatively) of African American science fiction writers such as Samuel R. Delany and Octavia Butler. I suspect that the reason for its neglect was the chaste nature of the Sun Ra approved edit, which took away many of the cinematic pleasures of the original cut, bordello- heavy as they might be. Sun Ra of course repeatedly admitted that he was very successful at being a failure; Ra's censorship of John Coney's film was arguably penny wise and pound foolish. What remains is a genuine cult film of lasting curiosity and entertainment value — especially in this pristine preservation.

Perhaps unfairly, I have relegated writings by and about Sun Ra to the conclusion of this afterward follwing the sounds and the visions. One additional complication here is that I have refrained from discussing the four audio volumes of Sun Ra's "space poetry" with modest musical accompaniment until now (on vinyl and streaming services, but not CD). They seemed a better fit with the writings, especially since there is some overlap between the Kicks Books paperback writings and the Norton Records vinyl (two branches of the same NYC - based enterprise). Michael D. Anderson was involved with both of these projects, as well as the mammoth box set described above, in his capacity as Executive Director of the Sun Ra Music Archive.

Paul Youngquist's *A Pure Solar World: Sun Ra and the Birth of Afrofuturism* (University of Texas, 2014) is a good supplement to John Szwed's biography, a walk through the life with an eye towards additional cultural contexts that illuminate Sun Ra's project. I think its greatest achievement is a very clear concentration on the importance of Ra's space poetry (in chapter 8, "Immeasurable Equation"). Youngquist gets at the heart of the matter by getting us to ask the right questions about what Sun Ra was up to:

> Whereas conventional Western poetry celebrates particulars and eschews generalizations, his does just the opposite, dissolving differences into abstract equivalence. His poetry of tone presses beyond perceived distinctions to reveal spiritual prospects that exceed them. Equations, not ideological convictions, set the terms for the social agenda Sun Ra pursues through creativity. The purpose of his tone poetry is to rediscover and resuscitate a life of spirit that exceeds everyday sensation and its workaday words.
>
> Not literature, then, but mathematics provides a model for this kind of poetry. (85)

Despite some family resemblances with Stephen Crane and Gertrude Stein that I have considered above, Ra's closest predecessors in their abstraction were — only in some of their writings to be sure – Age of Reason poets such as Samuel Johnson and Alexander Pope, especially when they were using heroic couplets as a venue for philosophizing (Johnson's "On the Vanity of Human Wishes," Pope's "An Essay on Criticism"). But as Youngquist notes, Ra's intentions were "spiritual" not "ideological" (as was arguably the case for Johnson and Pope). Furthermore, Ra's template for proceeding derived from a rather fanciful and metaphorical notion of the mathematical equation.

One of Sun Ra's cornerstone beliefs was that the fall of the Biblical Tower of Babel separated concepts once linked in a universal language into separate words in different languages. As a result, puns are as revealing for Sun Ra as they were for Sigmund Freud: not because of their being a gateway to the unconscious, but because they reveal obscured truths hidden by Babel's linguistic fall. As Ra's writings abundantly indicate, he took phonetic resemblances between words and morphemes very seriously as a key to hidden meaning: rights / rites, Negro / necro, birth / berth / be-Earthed etc. etc. etc. What linked Sun Ra's writings and his music was a belief in both of the salvific nature of SOUND itself. Sound shall set you free. Youngquist helps us see this. And again, this is Ra's doctrine – you don't have to share it if you don't want to. But this explains why literary critics and nit-picking etymologists who might wish to refute Ra's paranoumasia are both utterly missing his point, which indeed is his belief.

Viewed in this light, Hans Falb's liner notes for the Nickelsdorf concert CD are incredibly insightful. After all, the two creative artists of our recent time who most thoroughly paid attention to the pun were James Joyce in *Finnegans Wake* and Arno Schmidt in *Zettel's Traum / Bottom's Dream* (where for ca. 1500 huge pages of his novel Schmidt dissects the writings of Edgar Allan Poe by using what he calls a search for "etyms," echoes of meaning discernible in similar phonetic sounds — interpretation by / as punning).

The other two major Sun Ra publication updates are two volumes of his "science fiction poetry" and spoken pronouncements: *This Planet Is Doomed* (2011) and *Prophetika: Book One* (2014). Both are published by Kicks Books ("Good Reading for the Minions") in tandem with four vinyl / MP3 / streaming spoken word releases of Sun Ra's verse: *Strange Worlds in my Mind, The Sub-Dwellers, The Outer Darkness* and *My Way is the Spaceways*. It must be noted that these are all posthumous releases: although Sun Ra sold his poetry in various versions from the band stand or by mail order as *The Immeasurable Equation*, these works were not released as such in his lifetime.

Their legitimacy is indisputable, however, and they will reinforce anything I have previously said about Sun Ra's beliefs. For example, the Tower of Babel shows up in "the universe is out there waiting": "I'm afraid to tell you / who confused the languages, but... / GOD DID!" (*Prophetika* 44). And a recurrent suspicion of bodily drives in the poetry suggests Sun Ra's own asexual tendencies: "I can't let them do it / like all these squares... / runnin' after all this / sex stuff" (*This Planet* 3). The source of these texts seems to be a mixture of hitherto unpublished manuscripts, the poem texts on the spoken word recordings and various sermons given in concert (which may of course have origins in manuscript versions). Sun Ra's poetry was anthologized previously by Amiri Baraka in his 1968 anthology *Black Fire*; it undoubtedly deserves a niche, albeit minor, in the canon of American poetry. His very best poems such as "tomorrow's realm" (aka "I'll Wait for You") have a way of lingering in the mind (*This Planet* 113).

In summary, Sun Ra's newly available artistry runs the gamut from the Hambone Kids to the sonic shocks of *Thunder of the Gods* — with the director's cut of *Space Is the Place* falling pretty much exactly in the middle. These new old works remind us that Sun Ra was a musician and a thinker not afraid to plumb the deepest mysteries of human existence from the perspective and persona of an extraterrestrial. Like Christ, who was both an inspiration for Ra and a worthy foe, Sun Ra spoke in parables. In some ways, Sun Ra was not only a living myth but a walking parable. No wonder he continues to draw us into his orbit.

www.ingramcontent.com/pod-product-compliance
Lightning Source LLC
Chambersburg PA
CBHW050318120526
44592CB00014B/1959